W9-COS-681

NF/Good
$6
1st ed Stated
65751

GIFTS FROM THE BIBLE

ENNEN REAVES HALL

Drawings by Ismar David

HARPER & ROW, PUBLISHERS

NEW YORK, EVANSTON, AND LONDON

GIFTS
FROM THE
BIBLE

GIFTS FROM THE BIBLE. Copyright © 1968 by Ennen Reaves Hall. Printed in the United States of America. All rights reserved. No part of this book may be used or reproduced in any manner whatsoever without written permission except in the case of brief quotations embodied in critical articles and reviews. For information address Harper & Row, Publishers, Incorporated, 49 East 33rd Street, New York, N. Y. 10016.

FIRST EDITION

Library of Congress Catalog Card Number: 68-11734
Designed by The Etheredges

CONTENTS

All scripture is given by inspiration of God, and is profitable. . . . 2 TIMOTHY 3:16

GIFTS FROM THE BIBLE

FOREWORD

Like most parents of his generation, my father denied himself many comforts and pleasures in his intense desire to "leave something" to his children. The property he managed to accumulate, however, would be relatively small in the unstable, inflationary markets of today.

As one of his eight heirs, I feel that I alone inherited something of priceless, unchanging value, for I was given his Bible.

It was old, the leatherette binding broken and crumbling at the edges, the pages dog-eared and soiled with time and use. Yet as I looked at it, I knew that it would guide me to the beaten paths over rough, mountainous terrain and that I would never get lost if I followed the trail it blazed.

How could land and money compare with the security such a book gave me?

Now, nearing the end of my own earth journey, I find that I, too, long to leave something to my children . . . to my friends . . . to the world. Although I shall leave no tangible assets, I have a priceless collection of rare items I would like to bequeath to whoever will be enriched by receiving them. These are entailed gifts left me for my lifespan only and on condition that I share them with anyone who may be helped by them. Like all rare and beautiful things in life, each has become more valuable with time, each more treasured with use. So it is my deep, deep joy to bequeath them to those who will in turn treasure them, accepting the same entailed conditions.

These intangible gifts should appeal to those who like antiques, for they have been lovingly handed down from generation to generation. The original owners were the pioneers who blazed a trail of faith-living through the wilderness of hopelessness and confusion that had sprung from a godless ideology. These gifts bring to mind the "perpetual incense" that Moses ordered should be burned "before the Lord throughout your generation" (Exod. 30:8).

They also contribute to a constructive and meaningful life today just as they did centuries ago. As the Psalmist reminds us, "A thousand years in thy sight are but as yesterday when it is past and as a watch in the night" (90:4).

In listing these gifts, each one held up to let the light of time enhance its beauty and sturdy durability, I cannot feel deprived or impoverished, insecure or afraid of what lies beyond today. The path along which the Bible leads me is so firmly packed by the countless feet which have walked ahead of mine, so clearly marked by such gifts as these left as signs to point the way, that my heart echoes the words of Isaiah: "They that wait upon the Lord shall renew their strength; they shall mount up with wings as eagles; they shall run and not be weary; and they shall walk and not faint" (40:31).

We who wait (depend) upon the Lord God are rich because our

heritage teaches us how to rise (mount up) above conditions that hinder progress toward the good life God meant all men to live; how to be able to run without crippling weariness; and how to make seemingly slow progress yet not yield to a sense of defeat. The following pages record a description of my assets and my last will and testament, though I have every intention of living for many years to come.

The gifts described here are but a few of the number that make up my rich inheritance. They are exhibited to remind those who recognize in them the same beautiful meanings that have given them value to me, that they share in ownership already. These gifts may be intangible objects, but they convey tangible truths.

This inheritance is stored in the ancient, priceless treasure chest called the Bible. Because man has divided this chest into two compartments—the Old Testament and the New Testament—objects from each have been chosen alternately, not chronologically, to emphasize the similarity between the gifts of the Old Dispensation and of the New. Time has not changed God, nor has it changed the spiritual needs of man.

Scriptural quotations are from the King James Version.

ENNEN REAVES HALL

AN ANCIENT
MUSICAL
INSTRUMENT

Opening the lid of my treasure chest of inherited gifts, I reverently lift out a small musical instrument.

It seems to vibrate to my touch, as though the echoes of songs sung to the accompaniment of its plucked strings still live in its heart as in the hearts of all mankind. Songs of joy and victory, songs of repentance and defeat, songs of philosophical meditation —it has accompanied all these outpourings that voice the deep emotions of the soul and praise the greatness and the loving-kindness of God.

A rich inheritance is ours in the portion of the Bible known as The Book of Psalms. This beautiful, nostalgic, and inspiring collection of poems is associated with a Hebrew genius named David.

He is at once one of the most colorful and diversified characters in sacred or secular history, having been a brave warrior and military leader, a wise and benevolent ruler, as well as a gifted writer and musician.

Although David is not credited with all the Biblical psalms, he may have influenced or inspired the writing of many of them, during his lifetime and later. He undoubtedly composed psalms to be sung to the accompaniment of my musical instrument, a lyre.

This fact makes it valuable as a museum piece, or as a collector's item, but my joy in owning my lyre goes deeper than mere pride of possession. In figuratively touching the strings that once gave sound to David's music I seem to be in direct communication with him, and with the love of God that dominated his life.

Thus my lyre represents joy in living, happiness in praising and worshiping God.

This instrument, commonly referred to in the King James Version of the Bible as a harp, originated in Greece where it was called a lyre. It was lap-sized, of delicate structure, with a sound box sometimes made from a turtle shell. Two curving arms were connected near the top by the crossbar to which one end of the strings was attached. My lyre must have come into David's possession when he was a mere youth, for he had won some renown for his skill in playing it when, as a young man, he was asked to perform before King Saul.

Saul, a strong man with admirable traits, was faced with heavy demands almost too great to endure. He was embroiled in a war with Israel's bitterest enemy, the Philistines. Moreover, it was a trying period of transition for Israel, since Saul was the first monarch chosen to reign over the people. Currents and counter-currents whirled about the new throne until Saul was almost engulfed by them. When he became subject to spells of moodiness bordering on deep depression, his courtiers and men of state told him he was troubled with an "evil spirit from the Lord" (men of that day ascribed both good and bad to the One God) and suggested that an expert musician, by playing upon the lyre, might be able to drive the king's private demon away. Is it not amazing that only in recent years has modern civilization recognized what the ancients knew well, that music is of therapeutic value in treating the mentally ill?

The idea appealed to King Saul, who then asked where a skilled player could be found. One of his advisers said that the youngest son of Jesse, the Bethlehemite farmer, was "cunning in playing and a mighty valiant man . . . and prudent in matters and a comely person." Impressed by this recommendation, Saul immediately sent word to Jesse, asking that the youngest of his eight sons and herder of the family's flocks be allowed to come and play for him.

David brought my lyre to Saul's palace, and whenever the evil spirit tormented the king, "David took an harp and played with his hand; so Saul was refreshed and was well and the evil spirit departed from him" (I Sam. 16:23).

(Saul's nervous affliction may have been a type of asthma, for the Moffatt translation reads, "David would take the lyre and play music till Saul breathed freely.")

As I look at my lyre, I see pictures depicting the eventful life of a poet-soldier. First there is a pastoral scene—a green meadow, or mountainside, with sheep grazing contentedly or lying well-fed in the deep grass beside a flowing stream. Not far away a youthful shepherd sits on a boulder or a fallen log, his lyre across his knees, and sings his thoughts aloud to the sheep, the birds, and the small animals that abound in the area.

Although the sheep do not appear to listen, their restlessness is stilled by the timbre of their shepherd's voice. As long as they hear music they have no fear of danger, for they know he is near and on guard.

Long after his destiny took him away from his family's flocks on the Bethlehem hills, David must have recalled those days of peace with a nostalgic longing, for he wrote the beautiful and comforting 23rd Psalm: "The Lord is my shepherd; I shall not want."

The next picture I see in the polished wood or turtle shell of my lyre is the same youth, still wearing his shepherd's tunic, lovingly touching the strings of his instrument and singing much as our youthful folk singers do today. But now the green pastures, the boulders, and the silvery stream have yielded to the impressive splendor of a palace. The shepherd sings to soothe and quiet a king instead of sheep—a restless, troubled king fighting nameless fears, often complete despair.

Like the sheep, the man responds to David's youthful voice singing softly of the greatness of God. The harmony of voice and strings is both relaxing and invigorating. Saul's depression vanishes and peace returns to him.

The picture changes once more and I see a restless, troubled world listening to the music of David's soul. It is as though one were being led beside still waters where peace and new hopes return to the human heart.

My lyre actually belongs to all men in every walk of life. Many of them, however, are unaware of the value of this inherited antique and so have not experienced joy in its possession. To them I would bequeath my equity in this part of our rich inheritance, adding a special song to be sung in the heart as in imagination their hands bring forth the beautiful strains that David's hands once did.

To you who view national situations with fearful, troubled hearts, or who have situations in your individual lives that pose threats to health or happiness, I would give my favorite of all David's psalms and the favorite of many—the reassuring 91st. Read it with the same appreciation and joy of discovery that would be yours had I left you something of great monetary value. If you read no further than the first verse you will be greatly enlightened: "He that dwelleth in the secret place of the Most High shall abide under the shadow of the Almighty."

The poet here reminds us that it is the man of consistent faith who is rewarded, the dweller in truth, not he who is faithful only according to his moods. When we sing with David, "I will say of the Lord, He is my refuge and my fortress; my God, in him will I trust," there can be no fear and no danger if we sing in faith.

"There shall no evil befall thee, neither shall any plague come nigh thy dwelling."

What beautiful reassurance for the believer! David climaxes this poem by changing his point of view so that in the last three verses his inspired words become those of God's very promise to man: "Because he hath set his love upon me, therefore will I deliver . . . he shall call upon me and I will answer him: I will be with him in trouble; I will deliver him and honor him."

In bequeathing you this psalm, together with my lovely lyre, I am giving you the most valuable thing life has given me—absolute security in God's love.

To the confused who grope their way through darkness, I would bequeath the prayer David taught me to pray when I feel lost and uncertain—a prayer for guidance as expressed in Psalm 25:

"Unto thee, O Lord, do I lift up my soul. O my God, I trust in thee. . . . Show me thy ways, O Lord; teach me thy paths. . . . Let integrity and uprightness preserve me, for I wait on thee."

This prayer expresses David's own experience, for he knew times when he could not make decisions alone, when he did not know which path to take. Yet he could sing confidently in this same prayer-poem: "The secret of the Lord is with them that fear him; and he will show them his covenant."

What better gift could be ours than to be shown the promise of our God to keep us in all our ways?

To the lonely I would leave the beautiful 23rd Psalm, which is my great comfort whenever I feel I walk alone. Then I stop and listen to the echo of David's lilting voice, reminding me that the Lord is my shepherd and no good shepherd ever leaves his sheep alone. He provides green pastures where there can be no want; He speaks and the sound of His voice brings stillness and peace. Even though I must walk in the very shadow of death, I need not feel I go alone, "for thou art with me, thy rod and thy staff they comfort me."

The frightened sheep has only to lift his eyes to see his shepherd. In hours when the enemy called Loneliness threatens to overpower us, the understanding Shepherd invites us to feast with Him. He treats us as honored guests, anointing our heads with the oil of love until our cup (our very soul) runneth over with joy.

To those in need, the impoverished of the world, I bequeath the solution given by David in Psalm 34: "The poor man cried and the Lord heard him and saved him out of all his troubles."

Is David just stringing words together here, as a child strings pretty beads? Is he making idle promises? No. Again David speaks from experience, from a deep and unshakable faith. "O taste and see that the Lord is good," he chants. "Blessed is the man that trusteth in him. . . . The young lions do lack and suffer hunger, but they that seek the Lord shall not want any good thing."

Would that all people in our world today could make David's faith theirs!

To the doubters, the skeptics who can become wildly enthusiastic over adventures into space, and who diligently study to solve the mystery of the planets but discredit the divine Power behind all creation, I would bequeath the inspiring 19th Psalm: "The heavens declare the glory of God, and the firmament showeth his handiwork."

Why seek to find answers that ignore God's handiwork? Is not the world too wonderful to have been made only by freakish acts of nature? And what is nature without God?

To seek knowledge is good, but in giving this psalm of David I offer understanding of the knowledge to be attained: "Day unto day uttereth speech and night unto night showeth knowledge."

No matter how wise we are, or how great is our contribution to science, we can be enriched by making David's prayer in this psalm ours: "Keep back thy servant also from presumptuous sins. . . . Let the words of my mouth and the meditation of my heart be acceptable in thy sight, O Lord, my strength and my Redeemer."

To the young in heart, whatever calendar years you have lived, I would bequeath the lovely "Royal Marriage Hymn" of Psalm 45. It will remind you that the destiny of all creatures is to procreate according to their kind. Man, especially, has a sacred function to people the earth, for he alone was created in the image of God, the original Creator.

Our modern world seems to be losing sight of the spiritual side of sex, emphasizing only its physical side. In the divine plan for procreation it was God's loving heart that made the physical union of man and woman one of life's happiest and most rewarding experiences, yet it was never His plan that it should descend to the level of animal pleasure only. Perfect union demands a meeting of spirits as well as a mating of bodies, for only then is the relationship blessed as He meant it to be.

Love, a word greatly misused and little understood, blesses any human experience, for love is of God. Yet love is not love but merely an illusion we reach for, unless it reflects the Nature of God, the Source of love. That Nature is unselfish giving.

In his "Royal Marriage Hymn" David says the bride should go to meet her husband "All glorious within," and that she must "forget also thine own people and thy father's house . . . instead of thy fathers shall be thy children. . . ."

Old-fashioned? Yes, I am bequeathing an old-fashioned idea of the sacredness of physical union between the sexes, because it is one I inherited along with my Biblical gifts. Slightly old-fashioned in today's modern world, but rewarding, according to David, who further says, speaking for God: "I will make thy name to be remembered in all generations."

Psalm 71, known as "The aged man's prayer," I would lovingly bequeath to the twenty or so millions past the retirement age, many of whom feel segregated and unneeded in a world moving too fast for aging feet.

The writer of this psalm undoubtedly feared the disabilities age sometimes brings. Yet he knew how to overcome this fear, for he writes: "In thee, O Lord, do I put my trust; let me never be put to confusion. Deliver me in thy righteousness and cause me to escape. . . . Thou hast given commandment to save me, for thou art my rock and my fortress."

Here again we see the warrior, looking at old age and obsolescence as an enemy, and seeing a positive faith in God as a means of escape, not from time, but from the defeat of spirit and body that too often come with time.

This prayer also gives the aging a purpose for living, a place in even today's world that only they can fill: "Now also when I am old and grayheaded, O God, forsake me not until I have shown thy strength unto this generation and thy power to every one that is to come."

So both to the old and to those who see the aged as social burdens, I bequeath the Psalmist's reminder that there is a place in society for them if they will make this prayer theirs and dedicate themselves to the Psalmist's vow: "I will also praise thee with the psaltery . . . unto thee will I sing with the harp, O thou Holy One of Israel. My lips shall greatly rejoice when I sing unto Thee . . . my tongue also shall talk of thy righteousness all the day long."

These are only a few of the inherited psalms I would share with the world of chaos around me. There are one hundred and fifty in all, and each sings of the greatness of God. Before closing this clause of my will I would add two other psalms. The first can strengthen the weak, comfort the troubled, guide the erring, and calm the fearful. This is the inspiring 46th, a general favorite.

If I were able to leave millions to charity, to endow great universities, or to leave written words of philosophical wisdom, none of those bequests would equal in value one line given us in this psalm: "Be still, and know that I am God."

Be still, O hurrying world, I hear David singing. Be still, O burdened souls. Be still and know that there is a God who will be "exalted among the heathen," when He is lifted high above the worldly things we fear. He is not, however, separated from material things, for He said, "I will be exalted in the earth."

Last but not least I would bequeath Psalm 150 to all who call themselves Christians, yet forget to exalt God in their earthly affairs, or fear the threat of heathen powers. Praise, constant affirmation of what we say we believe, will keep us strong as a nation and as individuals.

"Praise ye the Lord. . . . Praise him for his mighty acts . . . his excellent greatness. . . . Praise him with the sound of the trumpet . . . with the psaltery and harp . . . with the timbrel and dance . . . with stringed instruments and organs . . . the loud cymbals. . . ."

A praying nation, a God-trusting nation, should rejoice! "Let every thing that hath breath praise the Lord. Praise ye the Lord."

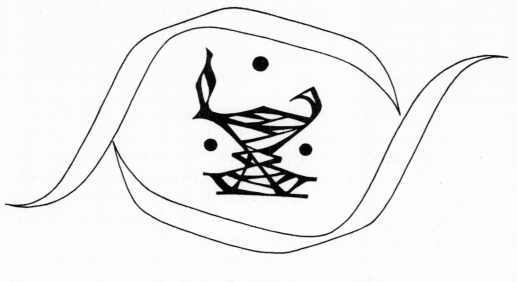

AN ANTIQUE LAMP

The most prized article in a friend's home is a lovely antique lamp that was once used by her great-grandparents. My home has such a lamp also, but it dates back even further into antiquity. Centuries and centuries further.

An ancient writer once said of my lamp, "Thy word is a lamp unto my feet and a light unto my path" (Ps. 119:105). Each time I read this graphic description, memory revives the picture of the oil lantern my father used to carry when errands took him out of the house after dark. Of course if he were living in today's progressive world he would substitute an electric flashlight for that smelly, smoky old lantern that only dimly revealed his path. Who can say what tomorrow's man may carry?

Yet there has never been and never will be a substitute for the lamp that provides light along life's spiritual pathway. Men continue to try to find substitutes, but these are merely imitations of the original. Much of our philosophy as well as our literature is based upon the Bible—the one Light that has never been improved upon.

The printed words in the great Book, however, do not really provide light any more than did the metal frame my parent carried or the plastic tube of the electric torch. The lamp or lantern of the past generation was useless without oil, our flashlight useless without charged batteries. In our spiritual lamp the printed words in the Bible are merely the wick. Love is the oil, and only when it reaches the wick does the lamp give light.

Even then it can be a variable light, casting shadows in some places, giving forth brilliance in others, according to man's manipulation of the wick. In the hands of some it may even become an unreliable light, distorting truth. It is ever a changing light, throwing illumination where each person needs it most.

Thus this timeless, beautiful lamp has for centuries been an object of controversy because of the position from which men view it. It is even contended by many advanced thinkers today that the light shed by the Bible is only an illusion. Still others turn the wick up only when they desire to throw light in a certain direction. An early-day minister was heard to declare that he could prove by the Bible that it was a sin to chop wood. When challenged for his proof, he quoted the words of Jesus, "What therefore God hath joined together let not man put asunder" (Matt. 19:6).

It is true that almost anything can be proven by the Bible if taken out of context. All the strict laws of the Pharisees, which Jesus often disregarded, had a Scriptural basis. Yet he knew they provided only a dim reflection of truth as he saw it because the lamp had not been kept filled with the oil of love.

The great American evangelist, Dwight L. Moody, reminds us of this truth. "The reader must have faith in the Bible, and a love for it, before he will receive much good from it," he wrote, and quoted

Pascal, French philosopher of the seventeenth century, as saying, "Human knowledge must be understood to be loved, but divine knowledge must be loved to be understood."

Only when the Bible is read in prayerful love, and with the mind emptied of preconceived ideas and selfish desires, can it become a meaningful, never-failing illumination to guide us on the path of daily living. Then it becomes more than just a frame for words easily misunderstood or misinterpreted.

This priceless heritage that is given all men can become exclusively yours or mine when we accept and use it in love. No one can rob us of this legacy so long as we cherish and care for it.

In Isaiah 62:1 the prophet describes salvation "as a lamp that burneth."

Centuries after these words were inscribed on parchment, a young man named Saul (later to become Paul) had an experience that illustrated the truth of the ancient prophet's words. All lovers of the Bible are familiar with this story in Acts 9:1–18. The zealous young Hebrew scholar was en route to Damascus to seize and bring to what he considered justice certain men and women who had left the orthodox Jewish religion to become identified with the "New Way"—those who believed the crucified Jesus to be the Messiah.

Saul was filled with what he believed to be a righteous hatred for all heretics. He was not yet aware that righteousness and hatred are directly opposed to each other, a fact he was to learn when a sudden, blinding light made him fall from his horse as though struck by a bolt of lightning.

Yet the blinding light was not what changed Saul from a vengeful zealot to a compassionate follower of the crucified Man of Galilee whom he had once hated as an impostor. Rather, it was the Voice that came almost simultaneously with the flash of light—a Voice filled with love for a misguided man: "Saul, Saul, why persecutest thou me?"

There were no threats of reprisal or vengeance, nothing to indicate the Voice as belonging to anyone other than a friend. That Saul knew the Voice to be superhuman is evident by his reply:

"Who art thou, Lord?" And by his quick acceptance of the answer to his question: "I am Jesus, whom thou persecutest."

Saul must have responded to the love he heard in that Voice, or he would have rejected this statement with scorn. A dead man speaking in an audible voice? Incredible! Yet it was happening, for the other men with him, we are told, "stood speechless, hearing a voice but seeing no man."

If Saul had any doubts, they would have vanished in the experience that followed. Struck blind by the light, he was taken to the house of a man named Judas in Damascus where he spent three days so troubled, so overwhelmed with fear, that he could neither eat nor drink. Then a certain Ananias visited him, one of the very men he had intended to put in irons and escort to certain death in Jerusalem, and this man also spoke with the voice of love, not hate. When he related how the same (supposedly) dead Jesus had given him an account of Saul's experience on the road and had told him to go to the helpless Saul, there could be no more doubts.

Then came salvation to Saul "as a lamp that burneth" and he became Paul, a wholly new man. He was no less zealous than before, except that now he was dominated by love instead of hate.

Today salvation is often identified with life after death, but Saul's experience, and that of many others to whom we are indebted for light, shows salvation to mean a changed life here on earth. It could even mean a changed personality, with new ideals and new goals. Love provides the light that reveals the way to Christ.

Many drivers of cars today can recall when night travel was hazardous because of undependable headlamps. The lights on those early cars were regulated by the speed attained, the higher the speed the brighter the light. So at crucial times, when safety demanded slowing down, the light necessary to reveal hazards became extremely inadequate.

This is not true of the Word that is a lamp (light) unto our feet. No matter how dark the night or how rough the road, it is consistent and dependable, quick to reveal danger spots and point out the right turns to take.

Yet this light, dependent upon the oil of love, is like those of the early cars in that the closer attuned we are with the divine (the Spirit that Jesus called God within), the brighter it shines and the more clearly it defines the way for us.

This is why my antique lamp has a prominent place on my list of bequests. It is vitally needed in our changing space age, when many otherwise progressive leaders are still relying either upon lights that fail at the most crucial times of need, or upon lanterns made useless because they are empty of the oil of love.

A BIT OF DRIED FRUIT

It may appear strange that I select this gift as important, but it has so enriched my life that I am doing just that. Strange, also, because I cannot even identify this dehydrated bit of fruit except to say it is symbolic of that once eaten by a woman called Eve; that it was the most expensive fruit ever known to man; and that the whole human race is presumed to have been cursed by her gourmet dining.

Popular legend identifies this desiccated, age-blackened, tasteless, and poisonous bit of food with the apple, though there is no Biblical support for this. Nor is there anything in the Scriptures to support the legend that the first woman's sin was the discovery of sex, as past generations were taught. Sex is God's procreative plan for His creatures, an important function that enhances both body and spirit. To see evil in it per se is to deny God, the Creator of life, in whose image man was made.

Many Biblical authorities relegate the whole story of the Garden of Eden to the category of fables, but whether or not it is literally true seems unimportant. The symbolism only is important. Although the garden itself may be merely a figurative place, as some claim, the story (of which there are two different versions in Genesis) illustrates a literal truth—that man's humanity is insufficient to attain the goal of earthly happiness planned for him by his Creator-God. Although he was given perfect living conditions— happiness, peace, security—he had not the human ability to preserve those conditions apart from his spiritual nature.

Land (the earth) is the divine plan for nurturing the body, creativity (attunement with God) the plan for nuturing the spirit. This indicates a necessary fusion of our two natures, the impossibility of separating one from the other and surviving. Adam tried it and in failing laid the blame upon Eve.

A widely accepted doctrine is that God expelled Adam and Eve from this idyllic life because of their disobedience in eating fruit from the one forbidden tree. If this is literally true, it seems to negate the great, forgiving Nature of God—Perfect Love. Did He not send to earth, through love, His own Son to restore Eden to man?

According to the King James Version of the Bible, God admonished that first couple, "Of the tree of the knowledge of good and evil, thou shalt not eat of it; for in the day that thou eatest thereof thou shalt surely die" (Gen. 2:17).

Eve's temptation came when she saw that by gaining knowledge she could become self-sufficient, and powerful like a god. "When the woman saw that the [forbidden] tree was good for food, and that it was pleasant to the eyes, a tree to be desired to make one wise, she took of the fruit thereof and did eat" (Gen. 3:6).

Not that wisdom is destructive, unless it is the wrong kind of wisdom, as in Eve's case. The tree from which she ate was not, as is generally assumed, a tree simply of knowledge. It was, rather, a tree of the knowledge of good and evil. So Eve, in seeking wisdom to "be as gods" (according to her tempter), acquired a recognition of evil in the perfect world God had given her. In seeing evil she began to know shame and doubt and fear. And because Adam proved weak enough to eat with her, he shared all the negations with her.

Thus Adam and Eve were not actually expelled by God from their garden of good as a punitive measure. They expelled themselves when they began to see their life, their relationship, and their God as less than perfect.

To see imperfection in God's handiwork is to doubt His perfect wisdom and love. To ascribe evil in any form to the Source of good is to see that Source as less than divine. As one New Testament writer phrases it, "Doth a fountain send forth at the same place sweet water and bitter?" (Jas. 3:11).

Impossible, also, for Adam and Eve to continue to find perfect joy and peace under conditions they saw as imperfect. Their act of disobedience did not alienate them from God as much as did the results of that act. The expulsion from Eden was the natural consequence of their own actions.

Because we are of the very image or nature of God, our thoughts are creative. They may create constructively or negatively, and our whole being responds happily or unhappily. Thus we create or destroy our own Eden through the degree of faith we have in God and in ourselves as His expression of love.

This power of positive thinking must have been in Paul's mind when he wrote to the Philippians (4:8–9): "Whatsoever things are true, whatsoever things are honest, whatsoever things are just, whatsoever things are pure, whatsoever things are lovely, whatsoever things are of good report . . . think on these things . . . and the God of peace shall be with you."

Peace! Is not this the desire of a war-torn world? Yet peace has never been stabilized since that first man and woman rejected it in favor of seeing evil; since they knowingly separated their humanity from their God-Self. In doing that they destroyed their peace and ours.

How can man regain Eden while following their example? That is the question my bit of leathery fruit raises and why I want to bequeath it to those I love. It is my prayer that they see in it not a lost Eden, but a challenge to help men regain the way of life God meant them to live.

Eden, historians tell us, has never been located geographically, giving rise, therefore, to doubts that it ever existed. Yet the Christian believer knows it did, and does, exist. Eden is in every human consciousness that puts such complete faith in God that there is no need to elevate knowledge above love and obedience and faith.

A
STONE
WATERPOT

This is a large, cumbersome gift with no eye appeal, yet I put it near the top of my gift list because of its important symbolism.

Cracked with age, discolored with time, it might have been dug up by archaeologists at almost any site where ruins of an ancient civilization were discovered. If so, it would have been recognized by experts as a waterpot for the ceremonial washing of hands in Jesus' day. Such vessels, usually holding as much as twenty gallons or more, always stood in a conspicuous place in every Jewish home, not only for use by the family but also for guests.

The Jews of that period gave much importance to the ancient ritual of hand-washing. It preceded any partaking of food or drink, especially when in public or when entertaining. A host who did not make it convenient for his guests to wash their hands upon entering his home would have been considered very remiss in social etiquette, and especially in religious law. The washing of hands actually had greater significance as a religious ceremony than for personal cleanliness, since it implied purification for the Jew who may have been defiled by contact with despised Gentiles.

Doubtless this religious significance caused Jesus to ignore the rigid social custom, for which he was severely criticized by the pious Pharisees. Once he was asked outright why he did not demand observance of the tradition by his disciples, and his reply was to excoriate the Pharisees for their hypocrisy in observing the letter of the laws of their ancestors but ignoring the spirit (Mark 7:5–15).

This waterpot, a part of my sacred heritage, is not treasured because it once held water for hand-washing. It has a greater importance for me because it once held wine. In my vessel Jesus turned water into wine.

In providing wine for his friends that day, Jesus proclaimed to the world for all time to come that ties of friendship are closely connected with the spiritual life he advocated, and that religion should enhance the joy of living rather than make people antisocial recluses.

Is it not significant that the Christ's first miracle was the providing of simple pleasure at a social gathering? It happened after his dramatic baptizing by John the Baptist, and possibly prior to his sojourn of forty days in the wilderness. Even with the weight of responsibility he had assumed at his baptism and with John's declaration, "Behold the Lamb of God!" still fresh in his mind, Jesus journeyed north to Cana, a village a short distance from Nazareth, to attend a friend's wedding.

According to John's Gospel, "both Jesus was called, and his disciples to the marriage" (2:2). Modern translations use the term "invited." Since an invitation is never compulsory, Jesus went by choice, both to enjoy himself and to give joy to his mother and their friends by his presence. Jesus loved people, loved being one of them.

Certainly Mary, his mother, took for granted his interest in the success of the festivities, for when she learned the wine had given out, creating a most embarrassing situation for the bridegroom and his family, she went at once to Jesus.

"They have no [more] wine," she told him, doubtless in a whisper to avoid being overheard. We can easily imagine her tone made the words dramatic, for the Jews, steeped in tradition as they were, took their social customs seriously. At a wedding feast, most important of all social functions, a bridegroom was expected to supply his invited guests (and often uninvited ones) with all they could eat and drink. Failure to do so branded him as either impecunious or miserly and brought shame upon his family and friends.

It is easy, also, to imagine the smile with which Jesus heard his mother's dramatic announcement. He replied, "Woman"—a term of respect in those days and often used as one of endearment—"what have I to do with thee? Mine hour has not yet come." Although the usual assumption is that he was saying he was not yet ready to perform miracles in public, he may also have been saying, humorously, teasingly, "This isn't my wedding."

Apparently Mary didn't feel in the least rebuffed. Going back to the servants, she told them to do whatever Jesus ordered, confident he would offer some solution.

Did she expect a miracle? Probably not, for no earlier miracles on the part of Jesus are recorded. Yet she knew her son was no ordinary man, that his heart was great with compassion, and that he would rise to the occasion in some way. She trustingly left the way to him. Are his loyal followers today always that trusting?

This small miracle, if miracles are ever small, was not only Jesus' first but his most inconspicuous. Without the guests being aware of it, he ordered the servants to empty the six huge ceremonial water vessels and refill them with fresh water. When this was done he told them, "Draw out now and bear unto the governor of the feast" (the M.C. in today's parlance). This the servants did, to the delight of the governor who called the bridegroom over to congratulate him on reserving his best wine until the last, a reversal of the usual procedure.

Although only the servants, Mary, and those disciples of Jesus who were present knew of the miracle that day, it was considered important enough to be recorded in John's Gospel. So too is it important to us still to recognize the concern of our Lord in every small thing contributing to human happiness.

No one would have suffered physically that day by not getting all the wine he wanted. Nor did the wine contribute to anyone's spiritual welfare. Yet there was enjoyment and harmonious communication between friends as hearts lightened temporarily. All because Jesus put his stamp of approval upon the happy mingling of friends when he provided wine for a feast the success of which was not his moral or social obligation.

So my ancient waterpot reminds me that my Christ wants me to find joy in the simple things of life, in worship and in unselfish giving. He received no applause for what he did that day, probably not even thanks from his host who may not have even known of the crisis Mary averted by appealing to Jesus. We today, like the Pharisees of that time, often do our deeds of kindness only when we are sure they are noticed and appreciated.

Often, too, we think worship of God calls for solemn faces, for muted voices, for quietness and possibly solitude. These conditions are sometimes much to be desired but more to meet our human needs than as a requirement for worship. Jesus, the Son of God, loved laughter. Then does not the Father, also? Jesus loved seeing smiling faces that reflected untroubled hearts. Then does not the Father, also? Jesus loved seeing strong bodies and coordinated minds. Then does it not follow that our Heavenly Father is worshiped by these conditions?

In bequeathing my waterpot to those I love I am bequeathing the thought that the Christian believer should live a joyous, carefree life. Those who have no God are the ones who are burdened and worried, too harassed by the cares of the world to take time to laugh and sing and play. They are leaders of a militant religion that denies the Power of God to maintain order in His world and direct men toward their own good. Let them use the instruments of force and violence; the true followers of Jesus have no weapons but those of love.

The wedding in Cana took place in the very heart of a troubled, conquered nation, tax-burdened and browbeaten by a pagan monarch. It took place just as Jesus was beginning his ministry to a world enslaved by fear, by political chicanery, by class discrimination, by religious bigotry. Yet he took time to join in festivities, and to contribute to the gaiety of an occasion that affected only a relatively few of the many, many he longed to help. He always had time to give love.

The happiness of even one individual, he knew, contributed to the happiness of a whole society. None of us are separate minds, but a part of a divine whole. Every thought, every emotion, and every act of one affects the whole. So no individual, no human need, was unimportant in his eyes.

Should they be in the eyes of his followers?

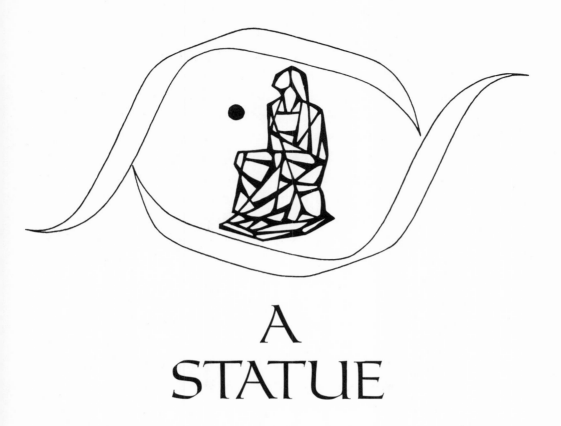

A
STATUE

This is a rare object of art, brought from the Orient—a statue of a heathen god. Although only a model, it is extremely valuable, for, like the original described in the Book of Daniel, it is made of pure gold. In addition to the exquisite workmanship of my model, it is priceless as an antique, for it was made by skilled artisans about 500 B.C. In its original form it stood ninety feet high and nine feet wide.

An ancient king of Babylon named Nebuchadnezzar ordered the huge statue to be erected, but my small replica became a part of my gift collection because of three faithful Hebrew men named Shadrach, Meshach, and Abednego (Dan. 1:7).

These three were taken captive when mere youths during the

Chaldeans' successful siege of Jerusalem in 597 B.C. Nebuchadnezzar had hand-picked the prisoners of war he allowed to live, choosing only skilled artisans, craftsmen, scholars, and the strongest and most promising of the Hebrew youth. These he carried back to Babylon. Unlike Hitler, he was not obsessed with race extermination, but rather with the unholy gains of slave labor.

From among the captive youth he selected the ones with the finest physiques and the highest intelligence. They were tutored in all phases of Babylonian learning so that they could read and write the language, and understand the complicated Babylonian system of numbers. They were also schooled in the social graces and indoctrinated in the heathen religion of their captors. Their courses of study probably also included astronomy and astrology, for the Chaldeans gave much importance to these.

By the end of three years, the wily king estimated, his youths were ready to become valuable court attachés. Possibly his plans called for sending them on missions to Jerusalem and other enemy capitals as ambassadors of goodwill who might succeed in planting Babylonian ideas within the hearts of the unsuspecting people.

The Book of Daniel tells about four captive youths whom Nebuchadnezzar found resistant to his plans. They were Daniel, Shadrach, Meshach, and Abednego. The king had not reckoned on the deep-seated faith and allegiance to their own God in these youths he proposed to brainwash. He was first made aware of their religious loyalty when the four refused to eat meats they had been taught were unholy, or to drink the rich wines offered them. Instead they went on a hunger strike, demanding a simple diet of vegetables and water. Because he valued them too highly to see their magnificent bodies weakened, Nebuchadnezzar had to capitulate on this point.

Later they met more crucial tests with the same moral and physical courage, though Nebuchadnezzar seems not to have abandoned hope of eventually brainwashing them.

My golden statue symbolizes moral courage, the courage that is based upon faith in God. Shadrach, Meshach, and Abednego (Daniel seems to have been away on a mission at this particular time) could be brave and defy the king because they knew their God was real, not a lifeless, powerless image such as the Chaldeans worshiped.

When the king had the huge golden statue erected, he set aside a day for the dedication and sent heralds throughout his kingdom, ordering all officials to appear for the ceremony. Musicians were assembled and at a given signal were to strike a chord of triumph. Then, at the sound of trumpets, flutes, and cymbals, all the people were to prostrate themselves before the idol. Failure to do so carried the penalty of a horrible death by fire.

It was undoubtedly a gala holiday, the narrow streets crowded with gilded chariots and prancing, jewel-bedecked horses carrying princes and governors and other important men of state to the site of the new idol. In the midst of all the excitement, three men must have worn troubled faces at the prospect of torture and death, for their allegiance to their true God would not permit even a pretense of worship of the lifeless statue, nor would they be tempted to compromise.

As expected, spies informed the king that while others prostrated themselves at the sound of the music, the three Jewish captives whom he had favored with education and high positions of state had stood upright and unresponsive.

Nebuchadnezzar, in his reluctance to lose his investment in the young men, yet bound to carry out his own decree, tried to reason with the three rebels, but to no avail. "If ye worship not," he finally warned them, "ye shall be cast the same hour into the midst of the burning fiery furnace; and who is that God that shall deliver you out of my hands?"

To which the three courageous Hebrews replied, "Our God whom we serve is able to deliver us from the burning fiery furnace, and he will deliver us out of thine hand, O king."

What unfaltering faith! What high moral courage! The king, infuriated at the complete failure of his attempts at indoctrination, ordered the three men thrown into the furnace. Then, perhaps secretly afraid of the power of a God able to inspire such faith, he ordered the fire to be made seven times hotter than was usually required to consume human victims. Then he and his other important officials settled down in ringside seats to watch disobedient men die in agony.

Strangely enough and beyond a heathen king's understanding, the men did not die. Instead they walked unscathed among the flames, causing the king to cry out in amazement, "Did not we cast three men bound into the midst of the fire?"

"True, O king," his yes-men chorused.

"Lo," Nebuchadnezzar continued excitedly, "I see four men loose, walking in the midst of the fire and they have no hurt. And the form of the fourth is like the Son of God."

Nebuchadnezzar was fully aware that he was witnessing a phenomenon beyond human explanation, and he cried out for the three captives to come before him.

When they walked out of the furnace, they were immediately surrounded by skeptical officials, who were soon forced to admit that the three were unscathed. Even their hair was unsinged, and not the slightest smell of fire clung to them.

A miracle. Yet such miracles are still happening where there is a deep conviction of faith in the power of God, and the courage to put that faith to the test. Many men today who are filling useful and important positions have been through a crucible that would have utterly destroyed those with no faith to sustain them. To quote the heathen king, "There is no other God that can deliver after this sort." Surely not his ninety-foot-high golden image, without life or the soul to love.

This image survives as a constant reminder that our God does have unlimited power where there is unlimited faith; and that unlimited trust should make us stand fearlessly for what we know to be right, to have the courage of our convictions.

Because of the world's great need for leaders with such moral courage, I would bequeath my shining statue to those men and women with political ambitions or dedication, with the prayer that it will inspire them to put ethics and ideals ahead of personal interests.

Also, I would bequeath it to those who must walk through the flames because of their allegiance to God. This relic of ancient culture recalls to mind the great part the living God has played in the advancement of civilization; how He acts through men and women who believe in Him as did three Hebrew exiles.

God did not deliver the believers from the flames, but rendered the flames powerless to hurt them. This He will do for all who choose suffering rather than deny Him.

Most especially would I bequeath my inherited statue to the youth of today. Perhaps no other generation in history has had to meet the subtle temptations to compromise which they face, nor has needed moral courage as they do. Those who refuse to yield to popular beliefs, or to conform to social customs or behavior patterns that are a denial of the ideals that have been instilled in them, refuse to bow to false gods. They may have to face ridicule, scorn, and censure, or even social ostracism, but they cannot be false to the heart's knowledge of God's laws, or lose the heart's communion with Him.

Only God knows how many unbelievers, seeing such faith and allegiance, will say in their hearts the words a heathen king once said: "There is no other God that can deliver after this sort."

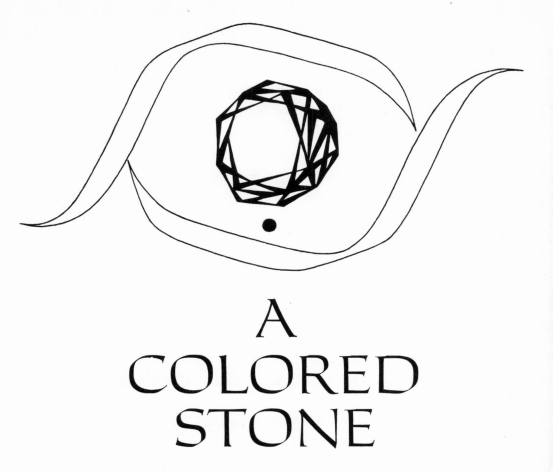

A
COLORED
STONE

Now I lift the lid of the compartment labeled The New Testament, searching for a gift comparable in value to my statue of gold. There are many, but the one I select is far removed from man's art, nor does it have any monetary value. Yet it tells the same story of faith and of moral courage that is immortalized in the example of Babylonian culture.

This gift may bring stares of incredulity, for it is merely an ordinary stone. Although bearing traces of color, it has no brilliance to give it eye-appeal or to arouse the interest of rock collectors. A close examination discloses the startling fact that the faint russet coloring is only on the surface and that it is not from minerals. It is only a stain—the stain of human blood.

Gruesome? No, beautiful. The blood is that of a martyr named Stephen, who chose death by unspeakable torture rather than deny his firm belief that the Jesus of Nazareth, crucified on Calvary, was the Holy Son of God, the long-awaited Messiah.

Thinking of the agony that was Stephen's the day my stone was used, I lift with reverence this gift he endowed with meaning for us. Then an inanimate object comes alive in my hands, pulsing with the love that lived in the heart of the man whose blood stains it. The writer of Acts (presumed to be Luke) describes him as "full of faith and of the Holy Ghost . . . and power," prerequisites to the type of moral courage he displayed.

It was after Pentecost that the new church began to grow in numerical strength and influence. There was some dissension at first about the distribution of food, for the members were attempting to live communally. With the selection, however, of seven men to oversee this part of the church program, the number of disciples, or believers in Jesus, multiplied. Stephen was one of the seven who might be said to have been the first deacons or elders of the New Testament Church.

Inevitably, the Jewish leaders became seriously alarmed at what they considered a heretical group. Stephen especially attracted their attention, for we are told that he "did great wonders and miracles among the people."

In order to trap him into making heretical statements, Stephen was maneuvered into a "dispute," or argument, but "they were not able to resist the wisdom and the spirit by which he spoke." Nevertheless, they charged him with blasphemy, seized him, and took him before the Sanhedrin, the supreme council of seventy learned Jewish leaders. False witnesses were paid to say they had heard Stephen declare that the dead Jesus meant to return and destroy the holy temple and to change the customs and laws handed down by Moses. This was the very thing the Sanhedrin feared.

When Stephen was asked if the charge were true, he offered no self-defense. Instead, he spoke eloquently and at length about ordinances and covenants made between God and Abraham and his posterity, even unto Moses. He reminded them of prophecies concerning the coming of a Messiah and ended his speech by boldly accusing them of having slain "the Just One, of whom ye have been now the betrayers and murderers."

They turned as one man on Stephen, but he remained unafraid. With a light in his eyes that made his face "as it had been the face of an angel," Stephen "looked up steadfastly into heaven" and said, "Behold, I see the heavens opened, and the Son of man standing on the right hand of God."

This was too much. They all rushed on Stephen and dragged him outside the city walls where he was stoned to death. His executioners, not wanting to splatter their clothing with his blood, disrobed and laid their garments at the feet of a young man, a zealot like themselves who was studying for the priesthood.

This man's name was Saul, who, as we know, later became Paul when he, greatly influenced by the stanch faith exhibited by Stephen during his torture, embraced the New Way himself and became the world's greatest teacher and evangelist since Jesus was crucified.

Although Luke may also have been there that day, I prefer to think it was Paul (Saul) who picked up the blood-stained stone we inherited. Certainly, whichever one wrote the account in Acts (6 and 7) gives an inspiring picture of a man, battered and bleeding, struggling to his knees just before his death to cry, "Lord, lay not this sin to their charge," then falling over into eternal sleep.

Praying for his murderers with his dying breath! How could one of Saul's mentality and integrity forget a scene like that? It must have haunted him, waking and sleeping, as he went about persecuting others like Stephen who adhered to the belief that God had walked among them as a Man, and had also died with a prayer for his executioners on his lips. Saul must have felt qualms of guilt that he had stood by and watched a man die without interfering, for when the same Jesus that inspired such loyalty in Stephen spoke to him on the road to Damascus, He said, "It is hard for thee to kick against the pricks [of conscience]."

So my incongruous and, to some, slightly repulsive heirloom, lying beside so many lovelier articles, speaks eloquently of a Power that changes weak men into strong, arrogant men into humble, cruel men into compassionate ones. It speaks of an inner glow in the true believer that cannot be hidden from others, of a rapport in Christ, a communion that makes it impossible to withhold praise and worship.

And it speaks of influential lives, of "signs and wonders" that follow disciples, of great endurance under trial. Lifting it tenderly in imagination, I balance it in my hand and decide there is no way to estimate its intrinsic worth or its value to humanity. Only God can do that.

Stronger than anything else, it speaks of the sin of apathy. The sins of omission—the indifferent attitude that left someone to suffer alone; the unspoken words that might have lifted a soul from despair; the acts of friendship never offered the lonely; the empty pew at church; the vote never cast.

Because I want the indifference of which my stone is a token to be heeded, I am bequeathing it to all the Sauls in our chaotic world—those who stand by and watch others being persecuted. With it I pass along the thought expressed by the writer of Acts: "And Saul was consenting unto his death." Consenting because he did not dissent.

That thought poses a challenge. To what evils am I consenting because I remain silent, making no protest? Are there crimes, wrongs, suffering that I could prevent if I spoke out, if I did something? To what extent am I responsible for the state of Christianity and for the state of the world? Am I one of those who merely stand by and watch?

Contritely, touched by Saul's pricks of conscience, again I touch a blood-stained stone and whisper a dying Stephen's prayer: "Lord, lay not this sin to their [my] charge."

Should not this be the prayer of everyone who labels himself a Christian?

A
BRASS SNAKE

At first glance this looks like a toy designed to amuse a child, but it has a far greater significance. It is valuable as a work of art, and as a relic of the period of time known as The Great Exodus, many centuries before Christ. Skilled artisans among the Hebrews molded it from brass or bronze ornaments collected from women among the Israelites, and upon the order of Moses.

Yet its real value is not in its craftsmanship, reflecting as it does the culture of that early period of civilization; nor in its intrinsic worth, much as the Hebrew women must have cherished their personal adornments; nor even in its historical value, priceless as that is.

The real value of this gift, our heritage from Moses, lies, as do all the gifts in my Biblical collection, in its spiritual significance. It signifies the belief that faith healings are possible, a fact often disputed by leading churchmen of today.

This inanimate object once healed thousands, although again we must recognize that the power was not in the object but in the faith with which the sufferers received the promise of God that all who looked upon the brass snake would live.

The story of how my snake was used as an instrument of healing is found in Numbers 21. The Children of Israel were encamped in Edom, resting from victorious skirmishes with the fierce Canaanites and mourning the death of Aaron, beloved brother of their leader. As usually happens, idleness bred discontent, then quickly fomented open rebellion just short of violence. In a body, men, women, and children confronted Moses, accusing him of having brought them out of Egypt only to die in the wilderness— forgetting that he had rescued them from slavery.

Their bitter complaints were caused by the shortage of food and water. "Our soul loatheth this light bread," they cried angrily, referring to the manna they were being fed.

Their angry protests only aroused new fears that now, in rebelling against God, they may have cut off even this supply of food. Because anger and fear are denials of God's love, they did temporarily put themselves out of reach of divine protection, and that night their camp was invaded by a death-dealing army of poisonous vipers.

Repentant, terrified, and grief-stricken, those who survived again confronted Moses. "We have sinned, for we have spoken against the Lord and against thee," they babbled. "Pray unto the Lord that he take away the serpents from us." How quick they were to run back to God when all other help failed!

Moses, his own hurts forgotten and concerned only for the people he was trying to help, prayed as they had begged him to and was told by God to have a fiery serpent cast in metal and "set upon a pole." All who came to look upon it would recover from the snakebites.

So my metal snake became a sign of healing, not only of their bodily wounds but also of their sick spirits. Those who looked upon the snake and lived must have been deeply repentant for their rebellion against God and against Moses, because we are told they "set forward." No people can go forward on a long and arduous journey in a spirit of rebellion and unrest and resentment.

How unimportant their first complaints must have seemed while they were battling for their very lives in the dark of the night, unable to even see their enemies, afraid to call upon God after turning on Him as they had! How relieved they must have been at the evidence that they were forgiven and still in God's protective care! How good that "light bread" must have tasted when they again ate in a spirit of gratitude! Many left their loved ones behind in wilderness graves as they journeyed onward, but we can be sure they went with light hearts, even though chastened in spirit.

Later, we read in the same chapter, the Israelites reached the place where God had promised Moses water would be found. A different mood prevailed. Gathering about the spot selected for a well to be dug, the people began to sing instead of murmuring and complaining and blaming. In unison they chanted, "Spring up, O well, sing ye unto it." Then everyone fell to work in a spirit of cooperation.

Picking up my glittering snake, I look at it and marvel at the length to which God has to go to make man aware of His love. There was no healing power in this brass object. No life. No love. Life and love are attributes of God, who had been supplying all the needs of the Israelites during their journey, and could have granted them healing without any artificial aids had they but believed. Yet God did not forsake them, even though they rejected Him. He spoke to the people in the language they best understood —that of idol worship.

Perhaps all the people of the Exodus had been born in Egypt where idol worship had infiltrated Hebrew religion to such an extent that they found it easier to have faith in a tangible object representing God than in the Invisible.

Perhaps Moses was saddened by having to compromise with Egyptian ideology and use a "graven image" to give reality to the God with whom he spoke freely, "as a man speaketh to a friend." Nevertheless he obeyed God, who is great enough and loving enough to speak in any way we can hear best.

The interesting and meaningful aspect of the story is that looking upon the brass snake produced healing because the sick looked in faith, not actually faith in the artificial snake, but faith in the belief that God, who had ordered it, had endowed it with some magic power to heal. Who can say He had not?

Another interesting fact is that my snake, although used as an emblem of healing, was actually the image of the evil from which the fear-crazed Israelites prayed to be saved. God used it to show the people that the thing they feared and suffered from was only an illusion, with no power to hurt them except as they gave it faith through fear. Nor could it help them except as they had faith in it.

The magic, then, is in believing. Beautiful healing magic—or black, destructive magic. So this gift sounds a warning to us to be sure of that in which we place our faith, accepting nothing but God's perfect good. Faith in the power of adversity will bring things to pass as effectively as faith in the power of God's love. The choice is ours. It is a challenging thought.

I therefore will this deceptively beautiful work in metal to those who are fearfully accepting lack or suffering in their lives. May they look upon it and recall another emblem of healing—a Savior nailed to a cross, lifted high against the sky for all men of all time to see. And the same God who spoke to the Israelites through Moses, says to us, "Every one . . . when he looketh upon it shall live."

Shall live if he looks in faith and love. Shall live a productive life, filled with that Savior's constantly renewed strength, his invigorating joy.

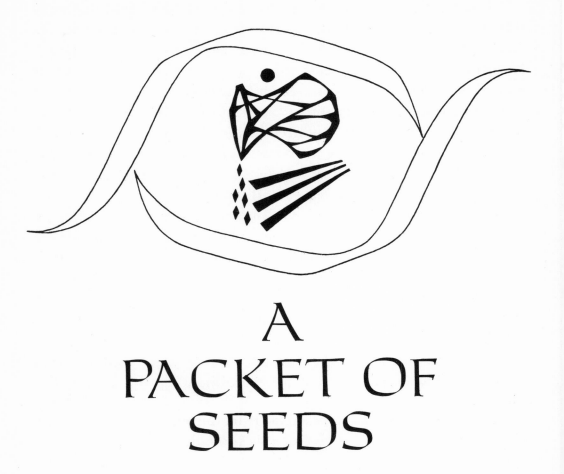

A
PACKET OF
SEEDS

Among my actual souvenirs is a gold pin, from which dangles a little glass ball on a chain. Embedded in the center of the ball is a tiny seed—a token of faith. A few years ago the wearing of such symbols was popular in religious circles.

Looking into the New Testament side of my treasure chest, I find a whole packet of such small seed, called mustard seed by Jesus. Although the seeds are very dissimilar in appearance from my brass snake, the two gifts are so similar in theme that it is startling to realize how little progress man seems to have made in religious faith in thirteen centuries. And it is even more startling to realize how little progress has been made since the day Jesus taught that faith should be able to move mountains.

"If ye have faith as a grain of mustard seed, ye shall say unto this mountain, Remove hence to yonder place and it shall remove; and nothing shall be impossible unto you," he told his disciples that day. The specific mountain he was referring to (Jesus liked to use metaphors and similes in his teaching) was a qualifying faith. The disciples, who had been performing miracles of healing in his Name, were unable to help an epileptic boy brought to them by his father. This was not because their faith was smaller than a grain of mustard seed, as is often interpreted, but because of their fixed belief that epilepsy was a condition beyond their power to help. A mountain too big for faith to remove.

The general belief at that time (and until fairly recently among certain people) was that an epileptic was demon-possessed. Superstition linked the sufferer's attacks with the phases of the moon and he was said to be moonstruck. Hence the sufferer aroused fear and revulsion rather than compassion, and the disciples reacted similarly.

They were doubtless unconscious of their reaction, for they were genuinely puzzled at the failure of their efforts to help the boy. A limited faith limits God's power, and it must have been the recognition of obstacles that brought the implied rebuke from Jesus.

Looking at the seeds I hold, I realize I am holding life in my hand. Each tiny seed has within it the power of growth and reproduction. But if no one has faith enough to plant the seed under conditions that give it a chance to express its God-given life, it remains a dormant, seemingly dead thing.

Suddenly I feel the stirring of life in my seeds as if each were telling a story and singing a litany of praise to God. One re-creates the scene at the foot of Mt. Hermon in Caesarea-Philippi immediately following the Transfiguration on the mountaintop witnessed by Peter, James, and John.

The rest of the disciples had been left below. When the three with their Master came down from their holy experience, they found their nine companions surrounded by a great mob that had witnessed their failure to heal the epileptic boy (Matt. 17:14–20).

Is not this scene being enacted today, over and over? Followers of Christ fail to demonstrate their faith and the unbelieving world concludes that God is impotent. Parents of afflicted children cry out for help, making the prayer that the desperate father made that day when Jesus asked if he could believe in God's power to help his son: "Lord, I believe. Help thou my unbelief." A qualifying, limited faith. All too often dedicated ministers and other religious leaders who could strengthen faith, in which lies the magic of healing, turn away and make alibis for their own lack of faith. They say that people ask of them the impossible, that God no longer gives healing as He did in Jesus' time, in the time of the apostles, and in the times of Moses and of the ancient prophets.

As though God, the Eternal, can change. Is it not man who has changed? The Israelites could have mocked the idea of being healed merely by looking at a brass snake and they would have died, thus changing the whole course of history. The distraught father could have accepted the consensus of his world that his son's condition was hopeless, thus not inviting ridicule by asking help for him.

My seeds speak also of other incidents where faith in God's power to change conditions brought results. Matthew writes of one of Jesus' healing sessions: "And great multitudes came unto him, having with them those that were lame, blind, dumb, maimed, and many others, and cast them down at Jesus' feet and he healed them" (15:30).

None were turned away, none declared impossible to help. Jesus did not limit the power of God within himself. Neither does a little seed. It just fulfills its destiny. It just expresses God, as did the Son of God. "The Father doeth the works," he said repeatedly concerning his own miracles. But he gave that Father-God an implicit, unquestioning faith.

My seeds remind me of still another truth about the healing miracles of Jesus. He did not have any fixed modus operandi. Because he knew that his power to help people was limited by their faith, he used whatever method of healing would best call forth their faith. Like a good gardener, he studied the seed and gave it the treatment needed to produce growth and fruitage.

For one blind man he made clay by spitting in the dust of the road, then applying the mud pack to the man's sightless eyes; another he healed by putting his hands across the man's eyes; to another He said, without touching him at all, "Thy faith hath made thee whole." He had faith in the reality of God, instead of faith in incantations or the laying on of hands.

One leper had to be touched; others were healed by the power of suggestion. Jesus simply told them to go to their priest, as the law of Moses required, in order to be declared clean enough to resume their place in society. Although the lepers were not healed when they started, they undoubtedly were by the time they reached the priest, for by then they would have consciously accepted their healing.

One paralytic was told to pick up his bed and go home to begin a new life—a challenge to faith. Another was ordered to lift a useless arm—an act that required faith even to try.

Again the seeds I hold seem to speak, this time of the Now. This is an age of miracles, comparable to the time of Jesus. There are miracle drugs, miraculous new methods of treating diseases long considered incurable, new scientific research, new methods of surgery. Why are we so remiss about giving God the glory for these miracles? Why do we separate man from his Creator-God? Is it not faith that inspires the researcher, the scientist, the surgeon, and the physician to devote their lives to the relief of suffering and the bettering of mankind?

Without the sustaining power of faith we would have no polio vaccine, no victory over a killer called diphtheria, no mechanical and therapeutic aids for cerebral palsy victims, and retarded children would still be hidden away like something shameful, to mention only a few modern miracles changing the lives of afflicted children today.

Even epilepsy is succumbing to miracle drugs since the hopelessness and superstition surrounding it have been removed. The mentally ill are no longer chained like wild animals, and the "deaf hear and the dumb speak."

Nevertheless men dare to say that God is dead, powerless! Were God again to assume human form and walk among us He could only heal where He met faith. Invisible though He is, He still heals by whatever method our faith requires.

The seeds in my treasure chest fill me with an awareness of the pulsing of life within their dry husks. Because I once, as it were, listened to the heartbeat in a tiny mustard seed and found hope for my own afflicted, I would bequeath my packet of seeds to all such parents as the one who dared bring his epileptic son to Jesus.

With the seeds I add the words spoken that day by Jesus to his disciples, words that hold as much truth for us today as they did for them: "If ye have faith as [like] a grain of mustard seed . . . nothing shall be impossible unto you."

Nothing impossible! No mountain too big to move if we pray the prayer another parent did as he kneeled in the dust at the feet of Jesus, holding his tormented son in his arms: "Lord, I believe. Help thou my unbelief."

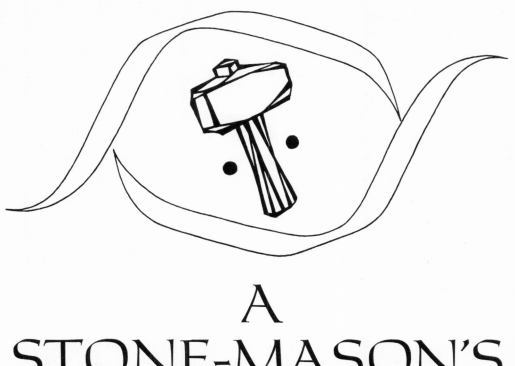

A STONE-MASON'S HAMMER

For this gift from the Old Testament we are indebted to a displaced man, a Jewish exile named Nehemiah, and a delightful gift his workman's tool is. At first glance, however, it may appear too commonplace and practical to be inspiring.

Lifting the heavy and cumbersome object, I am reminded of the truism, "God helps them that help themselves." Then I recall that this saying originated over five centuries before Christ, and has been thought by many persons to have a Scriptural basis.

Actually, the truism should be credited to a Greek slave, said to have written the original *Aesop's Fables*. These were children's stories noted for their moralistic endings, but they have lived on as literary adages. This particular adage read, "The gods help them who help themselves." Western culture has amended it to read God, sometimes heaven.

The adage nevertheless does have Biblical support of its truth. All the miracles recorded in both the Old and New Testaments resulted from cooperation between the human and the divine. Man called upon God for help or healing or guidance, and his prayers were almost invariably answered conditionally. Even the manna for the Israelites during the Exodus was provided with certain conditions attached. The ancient prophets were often given tasks to carry out which, had they refused, would have robbed them of their power. In the allegory of Job, a beggar praying for help was commanded, "Gird up now thy loins like a man; I will demand of thee."

In his miracles of healing Jesus instructed a helplessly crippled man to pick up his bed and walk; a paralyzed man was ordered to lift a useless arm; a sinful woman was told to "go in peace," which was equivalent to demanding that she reorganize her life.

In general the Bible negates the idea still held by some that prayers of faith result in miracles independent of man. If the Power we know as God operated in this manner, we would remain undeveloped and immature spiritually, mentally, and even physically. When need arises we can expect and receive effective ideas, physical strength, and spiritual endurance far beyond and above our humanity, but effort is still required of us. In a sense, we must answer our own prayers, conscious of God's help in doing so.

My stone-mason's hammer belonged to a man compelled to work out the answer to his own prayer. It was while Nehemiah, an ex-patriot of Jerusalem, lived in Babylon where he served the king as cup-bearer, that he worried over the plight of his kinsmen in Jerusalem.

A disastrous raid by the Babylonians in 597 B.C. had left the Holy City a shambles and Nehemiah longed to see its restoration. Moreover, he was concerned about the safety of the wretched people remaining in the city and the welfare of the new generation being born there. Although the great temple had been rebuilt, the protective city wall remained flattened, causing the people to be in constant peril from surrounding enemy tribes and even from prowling wild animals.

Nehemiah made the restoration of Jerusalem's wall his prayer project, with the result that he was, in effect, instructed by God to do it himself. The story, vividly recounted in the thirteen chapters of the Book of Nehemiah, makes fascinating reading. Written in the first person, which is a rare literary form in Biblical writings, and with a vein of humor, it is easy to identify with this ancient character and his problem. He could be the man next door, his challenge yours or mine. It is the oft-repeated, inspiring story of God using a little man to do a big job.

At first, Nehemiah tells us, he tried not to accept any personal responsibility in the matter. After all, he was neither engineer nor builder. His job as cup-bearer to a king was a lucrative and easy one, entailing nothing greater than tasting the wine before serving the king, to make sure an enemy had not managed to add poison to the cup. He felt he was doing all that could be expected of him when he petitioned God daily to send help to the people of Jerusalem. *Send someone, O God, but not me*—a not unfamiliar prayer.

The time came when Nehemiah had to consent, for his own peace of mind, to be used of God in any way He dictated. Even so, he was appalled at the idea of going himself to rebuild Jerusalem's city wall and help restore civic order. What did he know about such engineering projects? Besides, he was not free to go, he had no materials or tools to work with and no wealth with which to purchase any. An impossible task for him, he told himself.

Then he was reminded that nothing is impossible with God. When his master, king of the enemy country that had devastated Jerusalem, noticed his troubled spirit and invited his confidence, Nehemiah blurted out the truth. Instead of being offended, however, the king expressed interest and asked what he could do to help.

Nehemiah, feeling this must be God's hand at work, dared to ask for a leave of absence. Then he saw a demonstration of how

God goes before us to open doors when we commit ourselves to His will. Not only did the king readily grant him the leave, but he gave him letters to all the governors of Chaldean territories through which he must pass, thus insuring Nehemiah a safe passage. There was also a letter to the keeper of the king's forest, granting Nehemiah permission to take all the lumber he needed for his building project.

Furthermore, the heathen king voluntarily provided Nehemiah with an escort of soldiers to protect him en route from possible attack by tribes that preferred to keep Jerusalem weak and unprotected.

Nehemiah left the ancient city of his exile, with renewed faith and courage. Although his journey was without incident, he was made fully aware that his mission aroused antagonism and that he might have to battle enemy tribes as he rebuilt Jerusalem's wall. Yet he was undaunted and fearlessly tackled the problems that confronted him when he arrived in the Holy City.

They were many, he tells us. His first gigantic task was to enlist support from the residents, the people he had come to help. Want and fear and hopelessness had reduced them to a state of apathy, with no faith in their ability to better their plight. Again and again Nehemiah reminded them of God's covenant with their forefathers, and that his presence among them was testimony that God had not forsaken them. Finally his faith and enthusiasm became theirs, and he saw the day when they shouted with one voice, "Let us rise up and build!"

Build they did, in spite of all the discouraging obstacles they had to meet and overcome. Even the priests, he tells us, worked side by side with those who had once served them. Hunger and physical weakness did not stop them, nor the jeers of those who came to watch and ridicule, and to comment on their work, saying that a fox running up that wall could tear it down. And when enemy tribesmen came to stop them by force, even plotting to disguise themselves as workmen in order to strike from within and unexpectedly, Nehemiah had warning and outwitted them.

"Be not ye afraid of them," he admonished the discouraged workers. "Remember the Lord, which is great and terrible, and fight for your brethren, your sons and your daughters, your wives and your houses." This battle cry has continued to echo around the world many times since.

Plots and counterplots notwithstanding, Nehemiah, servant of a heathen king, turned to God for guidance and proved to be a great leader, an efficient builder, and a military genius. He made history by completely rebuilding the wall of Jerusalem in just fifty-two days, an engineering feat at best, let alone for one un-trained and plagued by interference.

In the light of Nehemiah's amazing story an ugly utilitarian tool becomes a beautiful sign of God's power and watchful care over man. It emphasizes a truth Jesus spoke over five hundred years later: "With God all things are possible [for man]."

Without God, without faith in His reality, Nehemiah's story would never have been written with the thrilling climax he gives us: "Also that day [the day the wall was dedicated] they offered great sacrifices and rejoiced, for God had made them rejoice with great joy . . . so that the joy of Jerusalem was heard even afar off."

Is there not a need today to rebuild spiritual walls? I look at my crude hammer, inanimate object that it is, which seems to be echoing the words used by Nehemiah in his early pleas to God to send help to Jerusalem: "Remember I beseech thee, the word that thou commandest [charged] thy servant Moses, saying, If ye trans-gress [Moffatt uses 'deal treacherously'], I will scatter you abroad among the nations; but if ye turn unto me and keep my command-ments and do them, though there were of you cast out [scattered] unto the uttermost part of the heaven, yet will I gather them from hence, and will bring them unto the place that I have chosen to set my name there."

Nehemiah did not need to remind God of His covenant. He needed only to remind himself. We do not need to plead for divine help to keep unity and goodwill among men. We need only to keep His commandments in our hearts. We do not need to pray for a

Nehemiah. We need only to pray as he did in the end, Here am I, Lord; use me.

If Nehemiah could stand before us to tell of his experience, I feel he would credit his success first of all to God's help, and second, to eternal vigilance. "Neither I, nor my brethren, nor my servants, nor the men of the guard which followed me," he writes, "none of us put off our clothes, saving that every one put them off for washing."

Vigilance, on guard day and night—such was Nehemiah's do-it-yourself way, a way, however, that was joined with prayer. This seems to be the timely message our inherited stone-mason's tool conveys.

Because this valuable tool becomes valueless unless it is used, I would bequeath it to the Christian youth of this generation, who seem more aware of the dangers of apathy and defeatism than do most of their elders. Not only would I place it in the hands of the skilled, but also the unskilled. The hope of the world, and the preservation of ideals and of the Christian religion, lie not only with the educated and highly trained, but also with those who are dedicated to helping their fellow man, those whose hearts hold enough love so that God can dwell there and act through them.

I would also leave Nehemiah's gift to the untrained and seemingly untalented church members, those who are faithful in ways that do not attract attention. They are true guards, entrusted with the responsibility of watchful vigilance. Men and women who see themselves as the least in God's sight can become the greatest. Does not Nehemiah's story prove this?

With this hammer I bequeath Nehemiah's philosophy: The cause is not ours, but God's. The power is not ours, but God's. Therefore He can use us to save lives, to save cities, to save nations, to save Christianity if only we lose sight of our limitations through seeing the illimitable power of His love.

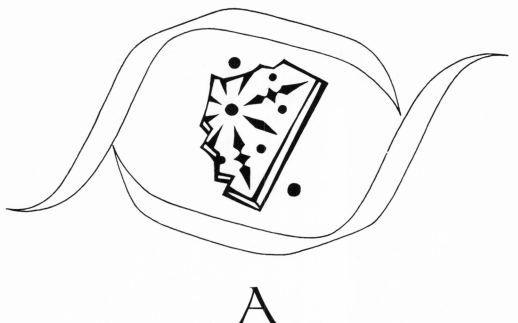

A
PIECE OF
TILE

Again opening the New Testament, I search for a companion piece to Nehemiah's hammer and find it, carefully preserved in three of the Gospels: Matthew 9, Mark 2, and Luke 5.

This object, too, may cause wonder that it is classified as a valuable gift, for it appears to be only a chunk of mud, hardened by time to the consistency of rock.

Let us look closer. See that broken end of a reed embedded in the clay? It tells us we are looking at a piece of primitive tile such as was used for building purposes in the first century. Actually such tile was not too different from that made today by the American Indians and Spanish-Americans of the southwest, except that for the reeds of the Orient they substitute desert cacti to reenforce the adobe clay.

My bit of mud tile once helped to roof a house, doubtless that of Simon Peter, one of the greatest men of all times. Does not that fact give it historic value? Yet it has a greater value in that it symbolizes faith and friendship and public service, as well as the same do-it-yourself way so effectual for Nehemiah centuries before.

The story of how my piece of tile came to be broken off the roof of Peter's humble home is yet another evidence of cooperative effort on the part of men who cared about their friends and neighbors.

Not only does the briefly recorded incident inspire faith in the power of God's love, but also faith in one's fellow man. It is one of the most graphic Biblical illustrations of how God expresses His love through the agency of men. It is also a pertinent lesson for today, when man's innate compassion for his fellow human beings is often overlooked and emphasis instead is placed on his apathy and indifference toward others.

The healing of the leper by Jesus early in his ministry was such an unprecedented medical miracle that news of it spread rapidly. So many people brought their sick or came for healing themselves that Jesus was forced to leave Capernaum for the solitude of the desert where he could pray.

Upon his return, he went to the home of Simon Peter, probably in the hope of finding rest there. Word of his presence, however, brought the crowds again. This time there were prominent men among them, Pharisees and doctors of law, who were actually spies sent by the synagogue leaders to catch Jesus in some teaching they could label a heresy. These skeptics came from every town in Galilee and Judea as well as Jerusalem. We are told by Luke that they were "sitting by" in the house where Jesus taught, having probably pushed their way in to occupy all the benches and crowding the small house to capacity so that the sick and needy could not get inside the door.

In spite of the hostile attitude of the important men, Jesus spoke "with power," and we can visualize how those unable to get inside the house crowded around it as closely as possible to hear the noted Man's words. Late-comers were simply out of luck. At this juncture there arrived four men, who brought a fifth, a paralyzed friend they carried on his bed which probably consisted of a thin mattress.

It is around these four unusual men that our story revolves. Four facts characterize them:

First, they were true friends. They did more than just offer words of consolation to an unfortunate man. They cared enough to do something.

Second, they were men with faith in God and in Jesus. Undoubtedly, they had watched Jesus heal others, accepting what they had witnessed as real, as divine. They believed.

Third, they were men of initiative and determination. They did not give up at finding the entrance to the house blocked. Their faith inspired them to make a way. The typical Palestinian home of that day had a flat roof with outside stone stairs leading to it. In the cool of the evening it was more comfortable than the close rooms below.

These four concerned men had the brilliant idea of bearing their friend to the roof, where they would tear away the tiles and lower him to the feet of Jesus in the room below.

It must have been an arduous task to carry a man on a bed up those narrow, steep stairs. Yet carry him they did.

Fourth, they were men motivated by the love that places human beings above law and above property. They were not, apparently, deterred by the cost of getting the man to Jesus, or by eventually having to pay for damaging another's house. So they tore up the mud tiling, making a hole large enough to lower the paralytic through.

How rewarded they must have felt when Jesus stopped his teaching to speak to the man so dramatically brought to his attention, pronouncing the word of healing they longed to hear! How happy they must have been as they watched the man who had lain helpless and despairing, pick up his bed, on which he had only a few moments before been carried, and walk out unaided, a healed and free man.

Both Luke and Mark write that Jesus noted the great faith of the four friends. My piece of ancient tile prompts the thought that intercessory prayer and acts performed in unselfish love and faith, are always rewarded.

No small part of those men's rewards that day must have been in seeing the changed attitude of the skeptics who had come to find fault and criticize. Luke writes that "they were all amazed, and they glorified God and were filled with fear, saying, We have seen strange things today."

We are not told that Jesus publicly commended the four men, only that he saw their faith. We do not know that they received any public thanks from the healed man, yet they had their reward. Love such as they evidenced asks for no credits or public acclaim, only the joy of service.

Another thought I would bequeath with this gift is that bringing men to Jesus is what counts, not the particular way in which they are brought. The result, not the manner of approach, is what matters. My way might fail completely to answer another's need, or his way to answer mine. If we come to God in love He can be touched because He sees the faith that inspires the coming. And the healing comes through that contact, not through the method by which we reach Him.

So, in passing along this apparently worthless gift I am in reality enriching all who will accept and treasure it.

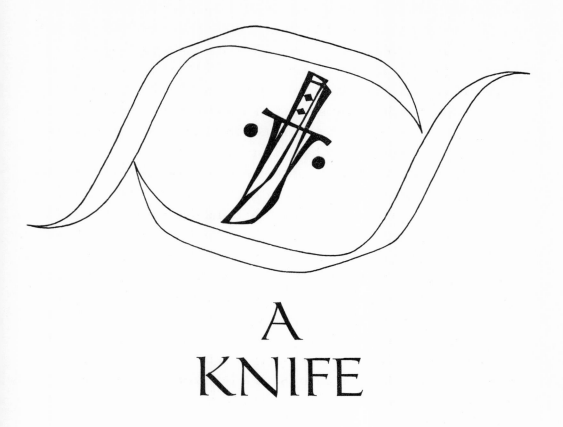

A
KNIFE

Upon opening the Old Testament we now take out a real museum piece—a knife made of bone which has been ground to a keen cuting edge. What might appear as intricate carvings on the handle are only the deep cracks left by time and the erosion of tears.

Any museum of natural history would bid high for this primitive weapon; I consider it priceless, for I inherited it from an ancient patriarch named Abraham. It is the knife he carried up a mountain in the land of Moriah, where he held it poised over his beloved son, Isaac, ready to plunge it into the boy's body if God so directed. Would that with his knife I could have inherited such implicit trust in God as that!

Although my knife is symbolic of a deep, abiding faith, it could well be labeled the knife of discipline for both parent and child— something greatly needed in today's world. Because Abraham in effect used his knife on himself before he planned to use it on Isaac, he has left us all something far greater than an instrument of death. He left us the key to happy and constructive living.

The Bible is filled with advice on child-rearing, given mainly as effective answers found by parents centuries ago to problems to-day's parents inherit. Abraham is one such authority.

This man, often called the father of the Hebrew people, typifies the modern parent who wants to live his child's life vicariously, who sees the perpetuity of himself and his dreams in his son. This dream began for Abraham long before the boy's birth. He wanted his name carried on, a proud lineage to establish a nation of people worshiping his God and living after his customs rather than after those of the heathen Canaanites among whom he lived.

A worthy ambition, it nevertheless denied Isaac his rights as a free soul with a divine destiny of his own. So the time came when the proud father had to yield priority rights to God as evidence of his faith. In doing so he gave Isaac a far greater inheritance than land and cattle, and to all parents he gave an invaluable lesson in child-rearing.

Although this story of the mountaintop experience of Abraham and Isaac is often used to illustrate perfect obedience to divine will, it seems just as illustrative of the wisdom of trusting our-selves and our children to divine love.

The legend also reveals much about necessary discipline in the home, of an ideal father-son relationship, of mutual respect and mutual security found in mutual worship of God.

We are told how Abraham heard the Voice of God telling him to take Isaac up on a certain mountain in the land of Moriah and there offer him as a burnt sacrifice to God in place of the animals customarily used. His explicit obedience to what he thought was God's will, in spite of his love and pride in Isaac, has been the subject of many written and spoken sermons, but com-paratively little has been said about the youth's role in this drama.

Isaac then was just entering puberty, an age which in those days qualified him for the responsibilities of manhood. He must have been as excited over the prospect of the three-day journey into the land of Moriah as most boys today would be. The two servants who accompanied them remained at the foot of the mountain appointed for Abraham's sacrifice. There they strapped wood across the boy's shoulders, then Abraham put his knife into his own girdle, picked up a brazier of coals to start the fire, and both father and son began to climb upward. Isaac was puzzled by the absence of any lamb for the sacrifice, but only upon reaching the mountaintop where they built an altar and laid the fire did the boy understand what was in his father's mind.

This mountaintop drama deserves examination whether or not one is a parent, for there are certain conclusions to be drawn on Abraham's parental role.

First, he exercised discipline in his home. Plainly, Isaac had been accustomed to obeying his father, for it seems not to have occurred to him to offer resistance or rebellion. He was stronger than his aged father, strong enough to carry wood that would have burdened the older man, and he could have resisted or run away when he realized what Abraham proposed to do. Yet he did neither.

Second, Abraham and Isaac must have had a relationship to be desired by all parents, for there is every evidence that it was love instead of fear that brought unquestioning obedience from the youth. He must have had faith in his father, faith in his love and in his wisdom.

Third, Abraham had given his son a deep faith in God, in divine power and divine love. As they toiled up the mountain, the boy had expressed interest in the ritual or worship Abraham planned. "My father," he had said, "behold the fire and the wood; but where is the lamb for a burnt offering?"

There was a ring of confidence in Abraham's voice when he replied, "My son, God will provide himself a lamb for a burnt offering." These words show that he had no real fear that God would demand the life of his son once he had shown willingness to obey.

Fear would have been a denial of his faith in God's many promises concerning the nation Isaac was to establish.

Fourth, Abraham encouraged his son to assume responsibility. He expected the youth to carry his share of the work load; he talked to him freely about their obligations of worship, and when the ram appeared in the thicket (the lamb he had said God would provide), we feel sure it was the strong lad who dragged the animal forward and who lifted the carcass upon the stone altar after Abraham had killed it.

Fifth, by his own great faith, Abraham discouraged fear in his son. He must have felt a rush of parental pride every time he recalled how fearlessly Isaac had allowed himself to be bound, and then watched his father pick up the knife meant to shed his own blood. And on the way down the mountain Abraham's heart had sung the words spoken by the divine Voice after ordering Isaac's release: "I will bless thee . . . and thy seed shall possess the gate of his enemies." Those enemies, Abraham knew, were everything that threatened the good life he wanted for his son, and they included secret fears and unholy thoughts and habits.

Abraham demonstrated that the first prerequisite for instilling fearlessness in another is not to entertain fears himself.

Sixth, there was strong family unity in Abraham's household. This is the picture drawn by the quaint phrase, "and they went both of them together."

Father and son worshiping together, walking together, talking together, working together. . . How could there be discord in that home? Not only did the son honor the parent with respect and obedience, but the parent honored the son by showing him respect and confidence. It was an ideal relationship.

Although Abraham did not leave his knife to me exclusively, I would like to bequeath my interest in it to the young parents who confuse love with indulgence.

Love, Abraham would say, carries an obligation to discipline pliant young minds, teaching them respect for authority as represented by parents, teachers, the law, the Word of God. Such authority spells security to a child. Has one the right to deny him that security?

Parents of older children will recognize the one mistake Abraham almost made as a parent and for which God had to correct him. In accepting his knife as an inheritance, parents also accept the lesson that was his and try to avoid living vicariously in their child. They see Isaac as an individual, with his own destiny to fulfill, his own experiences from which to learn, his own mind and soul to develop.

If Abraham's knife is used during a child's formative years, it will not be needed in the teen years. Then he will need responsibility, the sharing of family burdens, the knowledge that his parents have the faith in him that Abraham evidenced in Isaac. His parents will give him self-confidence and pride in his manhood by letting him know they expect only the best from him.

Parents of adult children will acknowledge the wisdom of the admonition given Abraham by God: "Take now thy son . . . whom thou lovest . . . and offer him . . ."

"Because thou . . . hast not withheld thy son [clung to your parental role]," God promises us, ". . . I will bless thee and . . . I will multiply thy seed . . . and thy seed shall possess the gate of his enemies"—shall live as God meant men to live, without fear because they put their trust in Him.

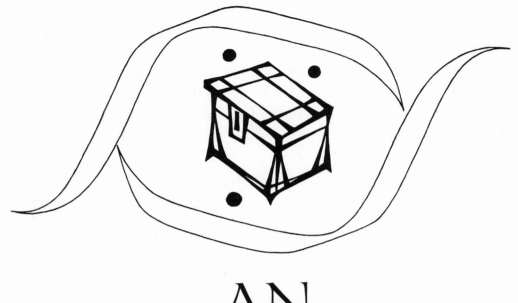

AN ALABASTER BOX

This beautiful little alabaster box typifies forgiveness. Its translucent whiteness speaks of the purifying influence of love such as Jesus gave all men, free of condemnation for sin or errors. Its delicate lines speak eloquently of the intricate nature of God-created humanity—perfect in divine workmanship but easily destroyed or damaged.

My treasured small box or flask once held precious ointment which a sinful woman poured over the feet of Jesus in gratitude not only for the love she felt in him, but also for his complete withholding of harsh judgment upon her that others were quick to give.

This anointing—a public expression of faith in Jesus—was made during a dinner party presumably given in Jesus' honor by a Pharisee named Simon, a common name among the Jews of that time. The woman was not a guest, but a social outcast despised by such self-righteous Pharisees as Simon. She had heard that Jesus was being entertained at Simon's house and she simply went there.

The fact that Simon made no attempt to protect his guest from attentions that would have been annoying and embarrassing to most men indicates his lack of sincerity in pretending friendship for the Man of Galilee. Luke says in Chapter 7 that when the woman rushed in and threw herself, weeping, at the feet of Jesus, Simon told himself, here is a test for this Jesus; if he is a prophet, as some claim, he will recognize this sinful woman for what she is and repudiate her.

Little did the Pharisee understand about love such as Jesus had for humanity. Although others would draw aside when passing her on the street for fear of contamination, Jesus did not see her as beyond God's love. He saw her weakness, however, and her great need for love. He saw her repentance, and her potential for good. So after he had rebuked his host for his failure to show him common courtesies, Jesus said to the unhappy woman, "Thy sins are forgiven. . . . Go in peace."

Was the rebuked Simon also forgiven by Jesus? Beyond doubt he would have been had he asked to be, had he shown any indication of repentance or of faith in Jesus' power to forgive. Since he didn't, he lost the opportunity to make peace with himself and to contribute to the rehabilitation of another.

Divine love, Jesus demonstrated, is not measured out proportionally as it is earned or deserved, but in proportion to the need for it and the acceptance of it. The parables he told of the Prodigal Son and of the Lost Sheep illustrate this truth. It was the erring son who had the purple robe and the feast in his honor, not the one who stayed home in a well-ordered existence. The shepherd left unguarded the ninety-nine sheep within the fold and went in search of the one which had strayed. Not that God's love is not the same for all, but only that varying needs demand different expressions of that love.

The teaching of forgiveness as an attribute of love was incorporated by Jesus in the model prayer he gave his disciples: "Forgive us our debts [our sins against others] as we forgive our debtors [those who have sinned against us]" (Matt. 6:12).

This plainly makes forgiveness from God conditional, for he further said, "But if ye forgive not men their trespasses, neither will your Father forgive your trespasses."

Why this condition? Not because God is less inclined to love those who harbor unforgiveness, but because there can be no harmony between a heart that refuses love and God, Perfect Love. Love must be forgiving or it falls short of being love, and to approach God while harboring ill will or resentment or self-guilt is to be denied the rapport found in divine forgiveness of mistakes and failures.

Jesus therefore invariably offered physical healing (a form of spiritual forgiveness) and spiritual enlightenment (a form of physical healing) conditionally. Such gifts rewarded repentance, which is a turning away from sin. "Go and sin no more"; or "Go in peace," have a similar meaning. True repentance indicates a changed heart, one freed of any attitude that denies love.

My two-thousand-year-old ointment container holds comfort for all who know themselves to be weak and erring. In turning to God, as did that sinful woman who turned to Jesus, we find, whether we are suffering in mind, body, or spirit, that He makes no distinction between the good and the bad, the successful and the failure, the law-maker and the law-breaker, but pours His love out on all who penitently wash His feet with tears, anointing Him with love.

Can we, then, claiming to be one with Christ, withhold love and forgiveness from the weak and bestow it only where it appears to be deserved? Can we withhold it from ourselves?

Can we pray in a true spirit of love and at the same time point a finger toward others as our enemies? When a heart holds forgiveness there can be no enemies, for it will not recognize anything but the similitude of God in all men.

In bequeathing this gift to my loved ones I would also leave the thought that it is not weak to love the weak. If this were so, then our God and His Son Jesus are weak, for their love is ever reaching out where most needed.

A ROUND STONE

There is a stone in the Old Testament compartment of my treasure chest that cannot be overlooked. Like the one we found in the New Testament, it has no bright colors to attract the attention of rock collectors, or any distinguishing marks to interest geologists. In appearance it is just an ordinary stone, darkened by time and rounded and polished by the tumbling action of running water. Its counterpart can easily be found in or near any stream, large or small.

My small stone is, however, far from ordinary, for it once stunned a giant. That gives it historical value, for if the giant had lived, the history of Judaism and early Christianity might have been changed.

As I lift the small stone, balancing it easily in the palm of my hand, I am aware that, like all historical objects, it carries a message. Regardless of age or circumstances, it seems to be saying, all of us have something to contribute toward making a better world, one safer for coming generations. God has a place for all of us, assigning us a destiny, a post of service that no one else can fill. To accept opportunities to serve is to experience fulfillment as persons.

It has so often been said that the difference between success and failure is the ability to recognize and seize opportunities. This truism bears repetition. William James wrote in his *Principles of Psychology*, "If one has not taken advantage of every concrete opportunity to act, one's character may remain entirely unaffected for the better."

A youth named David, living during the first Hebrew monarchy, might never have become immortal had he not recognized and seized an opportunity to serve his country and his God. He saw a giant that had to be killed and accepted the challenge, refusing to submit to fear.

The familiar story of David and Goliath is more than history; it is life. Not only did it happen yesterday, but it is happening today and will happen tomorrow.

You are a David, my stone seems to say to me. You daily face a giant that threatens to make a mockery of your Christian faith. Are you afraid to accept his challenge, as were Saul and his army of trained warriors? Or dare you go forth in the power of God as David did, armed only with this small stone?

I am no longer holding and looking at an ordinary stone, but at a symbol of faith and courage. Touching it reverently, I whisper David's declaration made so many centuries ago: "The Lord that delivered me out of the paw of the lion and out of the paw of the bear, he will deliver me out of the hand of this Philistine."

New courage is mine, for David's Lord God is also mine. He is also everyman's, and everyone has to meet and kill his own giants from time to time.

Do you have a giant that needs killing? If so, examine again the story of David. He has left us explicit instructions about how to handle giants when they appear on our horizon and taunt us.

First of all, do not be afraid, even when one appears unexpectedly. Hurrying up the mountainside that day long ago, carrying cheeses and bread to his three older brothers who were with the army of the Israelites, David had no thought of giants. He probably wanted only to accomplish his errand and return to his sheep.

At King Saul's encampment on a mountain opposite that of the enemy forces, the Philistines, the youth found utter confusion. Men valiant in other battles had been cowed by one lone giant who stood on the opposite mountainside, bellowing a challenge that echoed like thunder in the Judean hills: "Choose you a man . . . and let him come down to [meet] me. If he be able to fight with me and to kill me, then will we [the Philistines] be your servants. But if I prevail against him and kill him, then shall ye be our servants!"

Even as David greeted his brothers, Goliath shouted his challenge again: "I defy the armies of Israel this day! Give me a man that we may fight together!"

Fear crossed the faces of the Israelite soldiers. They said to David, "Have ye seen this man that is come up?" Whereupon he asked in amazement, "Who is this uncircumcised Philistine, that he should defy the armies of the living God?" Disturbed and curious, the youth moved to where he could get a clear view of the one who had thrown a brave army into panic.

Goliath was a formidable figure, about ten feet tall, and big in proportion. His huge hands could have picked up an average-sized man and broken him in pieces without even straining. In addition, a protective armor of brass covered his body except for his face, and he carried a wicked-looking spear. "The staff of his spear was like a weaver's beam and his spear's head weighed six hundred shekels of iron [twenty-five pounds]." A shield-bearer also protected him.

David learned that King Saul, who was prepared to battle the

Philistines, was unable to cope with what had become a war of nerves. For forty days the distraught Israelites had seen no action, having been forced to listen to Goliath's taunts, while farther back the Philistines just waited for them to break under the strain.

What could Saul do? He dared not send a lone man to battle the giant, for that meant certain defeat for the whole army. To accept the challenge was to agree to their terms: surrender if Goliath was not killed.

David, appalled at what he was seeing and hearing, asked why they were so fearful. His question brought down the wrath of his older brother on his head. "What are you doing here, anyway?" he wanted to know. "Why aren't you home minding the sheep? I know your pride and the self-will of your heart. You only came hoping to see men killed."

Nevertheless David continued his efforts to arouse courage in the men. Soon word of him reached King Saul in his camp. The king sent for David, possibly to ask him not to make matters worse by goading the soldiers, already so weak in morale. Doubtless he was further distracted to hear David say, "Let no man's heart fail because of him [Goliath]. Thy servant will go and fight with this Philistine."

A second implicit instruction David left us when we battle our own giant is, do not listen to negative words.

David's offer to meet the giant caused Saul to be as skeptical as the youth's brothers had been. "Thou art not able to go against this Philistine," he remonstrated. "Thou art but a youth, and he a man of war [experienced] from his youth."

David refused to be discouraged, but he could not go without the consent of the king. So he told him of experiences he had never revealed to anyone else for fear of not being believed—of how he had killed a lion and a bear with his bare hands when the wild animals attacked his flock.

He added with confidence, "The Lord that delivered me out of the paw of the lion and out of the paw of the bear, he will deliver me out of the hand of this Philistine."

What could Saul say to that? He was deeply impressed, and noting the source of David's self-confidence, he said only, "Go, and the Lord be with thee."

A third instruction is, put your faith in God's power, not in your weapons.

Though Saul used the phrase, "The Lord be with thee," he was not willing to rest his fate on that. Like most of us today who say we trust in God, he felt the need to supervise things himself. So he put his own protective body armor on David, a helmet of brass and a coat of mail. Then he girded his own sword upon the youth.

Wise beyond his years, David realized at once that he would only be handicapped as he clumped about clumsily in the unfamiliar armor. To fight his giant he must go as himself, not as another. Besides, had he not said that his faith was in God's help? So he stated firmly, "I cannot go with these; for I have not proved them [am not used to them]."

Then he took off all the protective armor and went to fight a giant with only his shepherd's staff and his slingshot, weak weapons with which to meet a heavily armed enemy. We can imagine with what trepidation Saul watched him leave. Passing a brook, David stopped long enough to select five smooth stones (such as mine), putting them into the shepherd's bag which he wore about his waist.

He would discover, however, that one stone would have been enough to kill his giant. God's help would be his because he had consciously accepted that help before he started out.

David's final instruction is, do not let jeers and ridicule confuse you or weaken your self-confidence.

Ridicule is one of the most destructive weapons known to man. Most individuals weaken under it and begin to doubt themselves. David's adversary tried to use it, roaring with laughter upon seeing that Saul had sent a mere youth, unprotected and unarmed, to fight him.

"Am I a dog, that thou comest to me with staves?" he jeered with obvious reference to David's staff. He doubtless expected the unarmed youth to take to his heels before their fight even began.

David's confidence, however, remained unshaken. "Thou comest to me with a sword and with a spear and with a shield," he shouted back, "but I come to thee in the name of the Lord of hosts, the God of the armies of Israel, whom you have defied. This day . . . all this assembly shall know that the Lord saveth not with sword and spear; for the battle is the Lord's, and he will give you into our hands."

With those words he took a stone from his bag, inserted it into his sling and let it fly. It struck its mark—the giant's forehead. The jeering laughter must still have been on Goliath's lips as he died.

No matter what the name of your personal giant, David's methods of dealing with him will work. Be his name Poverty, Unemployment, Ill-health, Treachery, or Retirement, he can be successfully battled when met fearlessly with faith in God and faith in ourselves as His instruments.

In the light of what David has taught us, the stone he used to fell his giant becomes even more precious. Because it has helped me also to slay a giant named Obsolescence, I would bequeath it to all the poorly equipped, the seemingly unprepared and handicapped who must daily do battle for survival in a world of giants, where there is not always patience or sympathy with either youth or old age; not always understanding when one 'desires to be himself and not an imitation of another, when one wishes to wear his own armor.

The young will take my stone and hold it close, letting David's faith whisper hope and courage. Remembering how handicapped he felt in Saul's armor, they will insist upon wearing their own, filling their own place, living their own life but living it to the glory of God. Only then will they know the fulfillment of the destiny God planned for them.

The aging treasure my stone, for there are still giants to be slain. When they go forth (and often alone as did David) to do battle against dependency, ill health, poverty, or other enemies, they will hear Goliath's jeering laughter echoing through the years. David, however, has left words with which to answer those who see age as a period of mental deterioration. They are taken from the beautiful 34th Psalm, which David could have written in his heart after he killed the giant that threatened Israel. These words I bequeath you, along with his stone:

"O magnify the Lord with me and let us exalt his name together. I sought the Lord and he heard me and delivered me from all my fears. . . . Many are the afflictions of the righteous, but the Lord delivereth him out of them all . . . the Lord redeemeth the soul of his servants; and none of them that trust in him shall be desolate."

If your heart can sing these words with David, you, too, can become a giant killer.

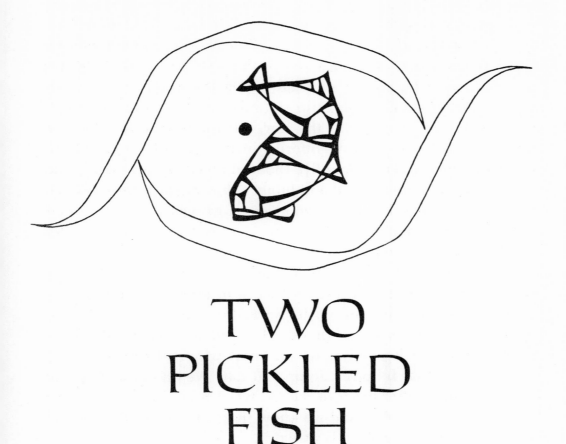

TWO
PICKLED
FISH

This seems an incongruous article to place in my carefully selected collection, and it is with a smile and an inner glow that I lift it out of the New Testament.

The smile comes at the thought of the young boy who shared his lunch of two pickled fish and five small barley cakes with a whole world, feeding each succeeding generation; the glow at the reminder of how Jesus can still take small gifts and multiply them as he multiplied that boy's lunch to feed five thousand—and many times five thousand since.

Looking at this inherited gift that time has not spoiled, I am reminded that the miracle in which it played a part is the only one recorded by all four Gospel writers (John 6; Matt. 14; Luke 9; Mark 6) and with slight variation in details.

Although it is one of the most familiar New Testament stories, again we find that comparatively little has been said about the nameless lad who played such an important role in that drama enacted on an outdoor stage in the hills near the town of Bethsaida. Jesus, of course, was the star, but the boy played the supporting role, for without his offering history would not have been made that long-ago day. And five thousand men and women would have trudged home so tired and hungry they might have forgotten the spiritual food they had been given. How well Jesus knew that body and spirit are inseparable, that neither one can suffer without affecting the other!

True, Jesus could have turned the stones that dotted the hillside into bread, but God does not work in that fashion, choosing instead to use human agencies for spreading His love abroad. That day (and countless other times) He used a "young lad." How young we do not know, nor do we know why he happened to be in the throng that followed Jesus that day. We do know that God can reach the tender heart of a child when more hardened hearts are closed to His voice; and we know there are no accidental happenings where His power is at work.

The lad had a choice that day. He could have thought with smug satisfaction of the lunch he had had the foresight to bring, taking it out as it began to grow late and eating it before the envious eyes of those watching him. He could have answered any request to share by saying, Provide your own, as I did; or he could have satisfied his own hunger first, giving away only the crumbs he did not want.

Instead, the lad offered all he had to Jesus (we can be sure Jesus did not request it of him). By this impulsive gesture of generosity he made it possible to feed a multitude that day as well as to set an example for all posterity to care for the needy.

Of course charity was not unknown among the Jews of that time. The Pharisees practiced it religiously, making much of alms-giving, and there was a "poor box" in every synagogue. No beggars on the streets or in the temple porches (and there were many) were ignored by the Pharisees. But their gifts were not always inspired by love; too often they gave merely from a sense of duty, or to keep the law, or from a desire to be noticed for their good deeds, or from fear that misfortune might befall them if they ignored the unfortunate. My two pickled fish remind me that charity given in that spirit demeans the receiver instead of benefiting him. Only gifts of love can uplift.

I find myself going back in time to that restful place where Jesus had sought relaxation for himself and his disciples after having just returned from missions of teaching and healing. It was, historians tell us, a green-carpeted glen between hills, and the human heart of Jesus must have longed to revel in the quietness and beauty of nature, to rest from the pressures that were his wherever he went. How often we long to "get away from it all" for even a short while! Yet, just as our concerns and pressures go with us, so did they follow Jesus into the hills that day. Although he had tried to leave Capernaum in secret, the word spread. Before he had time to relax, his privacy was invaded by a throng no different from those he had tried to escape. They came from every village along the lake front, perhaps even as far away as Capernaum, swarming over the peaceful glen like an army of locusts—the sick, the troubled, the curious, and the skeptical.

Yet what was the reaction of Jesus? Anger? Frustration? Impatience? No; not even patient resignation. The moment he saw need he forgot his own needs in responding to those of other people.

The disciples, of course, may have felt the natural resentments known to man. Certainly they were not inclined to play host to the throng. As the day drew to a close and the people made no move to disperse, Jesus brought up the subject of food for them. Philip reminded him, somewhat impatiently, it seems, that it would take considerable money to buy bread for such a crowd, even if there had been any place at which they could purchase it.

Others of the disciples urged him to "send the multitude away that they may go into the villages and buy themselves victuals" (Matt. 14:15). That was the simplest solution, but when they realized that the suggestion did not please their compassionate Leader, Andrew said, perhaps facetiously, "There is a lad here which hath five barley loaves and two small fish; but what are they among so many?"

They proved to be enough. Our little is always enough if we give it willingly and unselfishly. Perhaps the boy was too young to realize how inadequate his little would be when he naïvely offered the fish to Jesus.

The thought fills me with envy. Would that more of us could be what may appear naïve in our faith, not measuring our shortcomings but seeing God's power to make our little great. Would that we could, like our Holy Leader and the boy who served him that day, lose sight of our needs in seeing those of others!

This is why two pickled fish, aged but still appetizing, are worthy of being passed from generation to generation. They will never be old enough to be discarded, as such things usually have to be, because the message they convey will always be a reminder that all of us have something to give to the world we live in. It need not be great talents or great possessions; our little given in great love is sufficient. Perhaps it is no more than a smile or an encouraging word, but if it helps one it helps all. Who can measure the reach of the expansion of a soul?

In passing my fish along to the young on my gift list I would add a picture. It is that of a young boy walking beside the great Lake of Galilee on his way home from a day in the hills. The sun has just set and the brilliant afterglow, reflected in the water, matches that in his heart. His eyes are still filled with awe and wonder as he thinks over the events of the day, for he knows he has seen God at work. Even more, he has had a part in the most exciting adventure he could have imagined.

He starts running from pure exuberance, running and whistling and throwing small stones into the water to see the ripples spread.

How could he know he has started a ripple that day that will spread over centuries and centuries of time?

He only knows God has become real to him and that his world is suddenly a wonderful, exciting place in which to live.

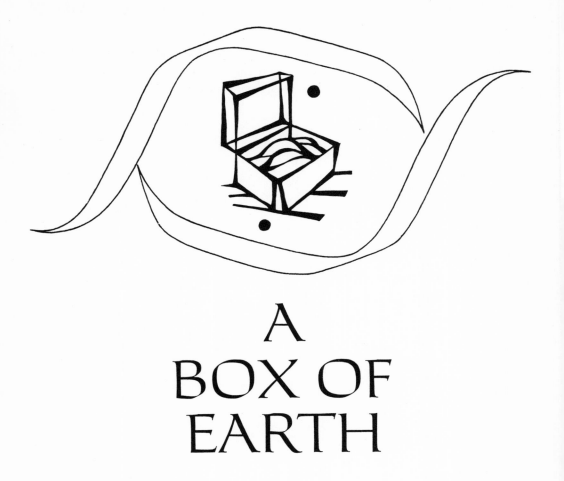

A
BOX OF
EARTH

Again I turn to the Old Testament to select a very special gift and, strange as it seems, find myself taking out a box containing earth. Just plain dirt. Can that rate as a gift?

Yes it can, for it conveys a beautiful meaning. It speaks eloquently of the spirit of brotherhood that must prevail in the world if men are ever to live in peace and harmony. It was bequeathed to us by a heathen army officer who wanted that message conveyed to succeeding generations after he was healed of leprosy by the God of his enemy.

Originally my small portion of earth was part of a larger amount, all two mules could carry, and the story of how dirt came to symbolize fellowship is told in II Kings 5 and makes fascinating reading.

The heathen officer's name was Naaman, and he was a captain in the army of the king of Syria, a bitter enemy of Israel. In a raid on Israel, Naaman had brought back captive slaves, among them a young girl he presented to his wife for a personal maid. When Naaman became stricken with leprosy, the loathsome disease that made social outcasts of the high and the low, it was his young slave girl who persuaded him to seek healing of the Israelite prophet, Elisha, in Samaria.

"Would God my lord were with the prophet that is in Samaria," she said to her mistress, over and over, "for he would recover [heal] him of his leprosy."

She said the same thing to her master, her pleas becoming prayers for the man who had so bitterly wronged her. God heard those prayers, made in such an unselfish spirit of forgiveness.

Word of the girl's faith in Elisha's ability to heal also reached the king of Syria, who had become greatly disturbed at the prospect of losing a dependable and able officer. He encouraged Naaman to make the long trip into Samaria to ask an unprecedented favor of their enemy.

Only a despairing Naaman finally agreed to humble himself by admitting he was a leper, until now his closely guarded secret, throw himself on the mercy of their enemy and ask for the healing magic they possessed. Neither the captain nor his king had any idea what that magic was.

Naaman's visit to Samaria has all the nuances of both tragedy and comedy. It was tragic to see the extravagant preparations to buy goodwill, and amusing to see such efforts to impress the enemy create distrust.

Naaman and his king wanted to give his visit every appearance of a peace mission. The king therefore loaded horses and chariots with rich gifts, silver and gold and expensive raiment. He also gave Naaman a letter to the king of Israel virtually demanding that Naaman be granted healing for his leprous condition. Then, as though to insure that Naaman would be shown every courtesy in Samaria, the king gave him an army escort, with all the pomp and display befitting an important man of state.

In spite of the gifts and his flag of truce, the arrival of Naaman at the capital of Israel threw the whole palace into an uproar. The king of Israel was stunned and mystified, since the Syrian king had failed to mention the prophet in his letter.

"Am I God, to kill and to make alive, that this man doth send unto me to recover a man of his leprosy?" he stormed, both in terror and in anger. "He seeketh a quarrel against me."

It appeared to be a grave political situation. An enemy had come bearing gifts, but asking the impossible of him, a mere king. If he tried to explain to Naaman that he had no such power of healing, would he be believed? Or would his explanation be taken as a refusal, giving the Syrian king just the excuse he wanted to send an army against Israel? Fearful of making a mistake, the king decided to entertain his visitor with pomp and ceremony, ignoring the fact that he was a leper.

When Elisha, the prophet, heard of the king's dilemma, he understood the situation and sent word to have Naaman brought to him for his healing. And now we see another drama unfolding. When Naaman went to Elisha's humble abode, he was still a dignitary on parade, expecting the same red-carpet treatment he had received at the palace. Instead, Elisha accorded him the same treatment he would have given any other leper. Without coming out to greet him and unimpressed by all Naaman's martial splendor, the prophet sent word through his servant that Naaman should go and wash himself seven times in the river Jordan, after which his healing would be complete.

The Syrian officer was humiliated and outraged, and considered Elisha's orders nothing less than an insult to his whole country. If it were merely a matter of personal cleanliness, he cried, Syria had plenty of rivers, bigger even than the Jordan. Why should he therefore travel so far to bathe in a river flowing through Israel?

"I thought, he will surely come out to me," he complained

bitterly to his servants, "and stand and call on the name of the Lord his God and strike his hand over the place [his infection] and recover the leper."

Plainly Naaman, typical of many of those who profess to believe in faith-healing, expected to see a dramatic performance. Perhaps he expected Elisha to go into a trance, or to show some indication of possessing supernatural powers. Naaman's limited faith caused him to place his confidence primarily in the manner in which Elisha invoked God's help.

Had it not been for the members of his entourage and perhaps the memory of a slave girl's earnest face, Naaman would have left Samaria immediately and doubtless another raid against Israel would have resulted. Instead, after much persuasion, he agreed to try the river bathing. The result was miraculous.

Looking at my packet of earth, I find myself imagining how this story could have ended. Naaman, after dipping himself five or six times and seeing no difference in his flesh, could have given up. We can be sure there was no evidence of healing until after the seventh time; not because there is magic in the number but because there is magic in the faith he must have found to persevere.

His changed attitude was evidenced when he went back to Elisha. This time he did not sit in his chariot and demand that people come to him. Instead he went into the prophet's home a humble man, stood respectfully before him, and said, "Behold, now I know that there is no God in all the earth but in Israel. . . . Thy servant will henceforth offer neither burnt offering nor sacrifices unto other gods, but unto the Lord."

Once any man feels the healing touch of God's love, there is no other philosophy or ideology that can satisfy. A little slave girl must have known this when she prayed for her enemy in his extremity and sent him to ask healing from the man of God.

Having glimpsed the power and felt the love of Israel's God, Naaman wanted to worship Him and remain within His love. So he asked Elisha for soil from his courtyard to take back to Syria where he would use it to build an altar to the Lord.

In this odd request we see a release of all animosity between two countries, insofar as Naaman was concerned. He had found a common basis with the enemy. Although God did not go to Syria with him in the hampers of dirt strapped to the backs of two mules, He did go in Naaman's heart.

I run my hands through the dirt that comprises this inherited gift, thinking how often the intangible is bound up in the tangible, heaven in the earth. God's first gift to man was a productive earth over which he was told to have dominion. Instead the earth and things pertaining to earthly existence dominate us.

God's second great gift was Himself, descending to our level in the form of Jesus to urge us again to have dominion over our earth. Yet we continue to let life burden and enslave us; continue to fight among ourselves over portions of earth that all belong to God. The earth, instead of separating us from our divine Creator-God, was meant to set us free as He planned for it to do.

Naaman's young slave was free in her heart, perhaps the only really free member of her master's household, because she loved all men, even those who persecuted her. Thus our holy soil, which made a healed leper feel close to God, reminds us of the nameless maid who prayed for her enemy, a girl who knew that God's love is freely offered to all men. She did not yearn for Naaman's healing because she hoped to gain by placating him, but because he was a suffering human being and she felt compassion for him.

So this box of earth that appears so worthless is precious as a visible sign of the brotherhood of man. Paradoxically, it is too precious to be bequeathed to any who value earth and its gifts above man, made in the image of God.

It can only be entrusted to hearts such as this Hebrew maid's— too pure to see evil in others, too filled with love to recognize any man as her enemy.

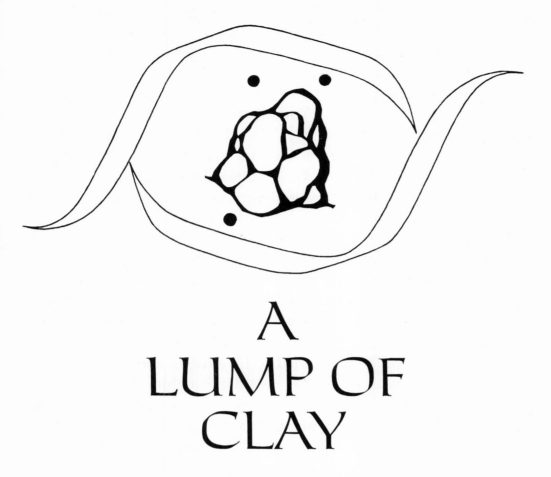

A
LUMP OF
CLAY

In the New Testament we find another gift of soil and lift it reverently, for this too is holy. Once it was soft and made a healing poultice for a blind man's eyes. Now it is hardened by time almost to the consistency of rock, but it is still simple clay.

It is not ordinary clay, however, for it was formed when our Lord Jesus spit in the dust of the road. As I hold it, I seem to feel love still vibrating through it and gratitude fills me that it has been included in our inheritance of Biblical gifts.

The message of this lump of clay emphasizes that the manner in which God heals is not the same for all, that only the contact with divine love is important. Four men broke laws in bringing a paralytic friend to Jesus; a slave maid influenced her owner hundreds of years before to humble himself before his enemies. In this instance no one cared enough about a man blind from birth, or believed enough, even to tell him there was a Healer in Jerusalem. So Jesus went looking for him.

What an exciting, comforting thought! God does not wait for us to tell Him our needs. "Your Father knoweth what things ye have need of, before ye ask him," Jesus taught, and demonstrated this truth the day he offered the blind man his sight. Neither the beggar nor his family had ever dreamed he would see. Yet Jesus must have known his gift would be accepted, else he would not have offered it.

The ninth chapter of John's Gospel tells the thrilling story that revolves about my clod. We can picture a blind beggar (all blind men were beggars in that day, for there were no other means of livelihood), sitting beside a road and making his customary pleas for alms, unaware that he was about to be given a whole new world because Love was walking toward him. We feel that even though this beggar was resigned to his fate, he must have longed to be as other men, to see the world about him, which he now knew only through sound. That longing was a prayer heard and answered by Jesus the day he and his disciples passed the beggar and they asked, "Master, who did sin, this man, or his parents, that he was born blind?"

Jesus replied that the man's destiny was not a punishment sent by God, as men of that day believed (and some today still do), but that God could be glorified even under such circumstances. Without asking the beggar if he would be healed, Jesus spat on the ground and made a pack of clay which he laid across eyes that had never seen light. Then he told the man, "Go wash in the pool of Siloam."

What love and what power that man must have felt in the hands of Jesus that he obeyed so readily, without argument or questions! He must have left his begging station in something more than hope, more than a desire to please a perfect stranger, for otherwise he would have been reluctant to lose the time and possible alms. He had to go in faith. We can imagine the upsurging of joy, of eager anticipation, as he hurried off in the direction of the pool.

No doubt in his haste he collided with others, bringing on vituperations, and perhaps he stumbled and fell more than once. But he kept on because he suddenly believed there would be healing ahead of him, and a new life, new joys, new accomplishments.

He believed—but in what? The power in the hands that had touched him? Or the clay spread like ointment across his eyes? Or the healing believed to be found in the pool of Siloam?

Perhaps he believed in all of these things. The magic was in the fact that he who had lived in hopelessness all his life now entertained the possibility of seeing. He really accepted completely the idea that he could be healed before healing became an actuality, otherwise he would surely have turned back before he reached the pool, reminding himself that everyone he knew believed congenital blindness to be beyond the power of man to heal. But perhaps he also reminded himself that it was not beyond the power of God to heal.

Later he virtually said this when questioned by Pharisees and synagogue leaders who tried to get him to deny that Jesus, whom they considered an imposter, a "sinner," had anything to do with the restoration of his sight. The healed man's first response was, "Whether he be a sinner or no, I know not; one thing I know, that whereas I was blind, now I see."

When they continued to press him, he gave another classic reply: "We know that God heareth not sinners; but if any man be a worshipper of God and doeth his will, him he heareth."

Then he challenged them to tell of any other incident in history in which a man born blind had been made to see, and daringly closed his argument with a declaration of faith in a man whose face he had never seen: "If this man were not of God, he could do nothing."

So my ugly little clod becomes beautiful because it represents faith in the Unseen, giving Reality to what appears to be unreal. It also represents the moral courage to defy tradition and custom and stand up for one's own convictions of right and wrong. The healed man paid a price for refusing to compromise and say what the enemies of Jesus wanted to hear. He was "cast out" of the synagogue, which was equivalent to excommunication and social ostracism.

This was serious punishment for a Jew reared in the belief that synagogue worship was of great importance. Even the man's parents, happy as they must have been that their blind son could see, had not dared to give Jesus credit for the miracle. When questioned by the Pharisees, they had given evasive replies: "We know that this is our son and that he was born blind. But by what means he now seeth we know not; or who hath opened his eyes we know not."

As I hold the clod gently in my hand, careful not to damage so sacred a relic, I think of how often parents today fail to take a definite stand where moral issues are involved; how often they lack the courage to live the principles taught to children; how reluctant they are to explore inherited religious teachings and how carelessly they pass these teachings along to the next generation without regard for the latter's peculiar and particular needs.

It reminds me, too, of how most parents offer children only a nebulous faith. They "know not by what means . . . or who . . ." If questioned, some parents have no answers to support the faith they profess. If loved ones seek and find a faith of their own, parents often sense a schism and are grieved. Although only an abnormal parent would accept physical blindness for a child without making every human effort and every sacrifice necessary to search for healing, countless numbers are content to rear them in spiritual blindness, offering no light to guide them through the pitfalls created by a pleasure-mad, commercial-minded world.

To whom shall I bequeath my small sacred clod? I wonder. Shall it be to the parents who have no definite faith to share with their confused children? Or to those children denied such parental counseling? Perhaps both groups should inherit it, for to enrich them would enrich the present world, and worlds yet to come.

I wish I could include with it the unshakable faith of a man who was born blind but was made to see; and his high moral courage in witnessing for God in the midst of skeptics. There is also the reward that was his the day he walked the streets of Jerusalem, no longer a beggar but still an object of public scorn. Before long he met the Man who had healed him, for Jesus had heard of his disgrace and came looking for him.

"Dost thou believe on the Son of God?" the stranger asked, and the man, who had never seen the face of his Benefactor, said, "Who is he, Lord?"

Then Jesus, who rarely proclaimed his divinity, answered, "It is he that talketh with thee."

What harmony there must have been during that street meeting! So much is left to the imagination in the simple terseness of the Gospel writer: "And he said, Lord, I believe. And he worshipped him."

No one can describe the unspeakable joy of recognition of the Christ, the rapport of communication, the first awareness that one does not walk alone, an outcast from the good life that is yearned for. When this same Jesus hears a cry of loneliness, he comes looking for us also, and then we know for ourselves how a once-blind man felt.

Does not this little lump of clay, therefore, represent more than a bit of earth? Does it not reveal a glimpse of heaven?

A
GOURD

This gift, found in the Old Testament, has many practical uses. Early American settlers fashioned dippers and other household articles from it; and in the American southwest today it is made colorful with paints and dyes for decorative purposes.

The man who bequeathed it to me, however, had still another use in mind. He wanted it to be a reminder of the universality of God's love, because a gourd vine was used by the Almighty to teach him that important lesson. This man's name is Jonah and usually he is associated with a whale, in whose belly he is said to have lived three days and nights. Perhaps he did, but I find that of far less interest than Jonah's experience after the whale disgorged him.

When Jonah finally accepted God's call to go to Nineveh, he went with great unwillingness, for he did not believe that God's love and care could encompass people of an alien faith such as that of the heathen citizens of Nineveh.

My gourd reminds me that the love of God extends as readily toward the "unsaved" as to the "saved." The only difference lies in awareness or unawareness on the part of the individual. Every infant is born a child of God, whether or not he ever learns to call upon his Heavenly Father.

So it is with reverence and joy that I handle my gourd and proudly display it as one of our most valuable inheritances.

Jonah, as has been said, was at first extremely reluctant to go to Nineveh, even though he was convinced that God wanted him to warn the people there of the certain consequences of their wickedness. Nineveh was the capital city of Assyria, hated and feared enemy of Israel. Jonah, a strong nationalist, wanted nothing to do with it and tried to evade the clear command of God by taking a ship to Spain, then the outpost of civilization.

When the vessel ran into a heavy storm, he interpreted it as punishment from God for his disobedience. How quick man is to lay his mistakes and guilt upon God, serving Him through fear of punishment rather than in love and trust! Jonah felt himself forsaken of God when danger threatened and fear took control. Lying in what appeared to be a dank, moving cavern, "he remembered the Lord."

What did he remember? That God is Love Incarnate, too holy to see man's faults? That God is law, always ready to mete out justice? To judge by his prayer, it must have been the latter, guilt adding to his very natural fears.

He prayed to the Lord his God, saying, "I am cast out of thy sight . . . they that observe lying vanities forsake their own mercy, but I will sacrifice unto thee with the voice of thanksgiving; I will pay that that I have vowed."

Too often God is remembered only when problems arise or when danger threatens. Then, like Jonah, divine protection is sought, with the vow never again to leave the consciousness of His love, to worship in thanksgiving. And too often repentance is as short-lived as Jonah's.

Oh, he went to Nineveh. But did he go in love for his enemies, in a desire to help them? Or was he not more selfishly motivated, hoping to win favor from God for himself, thereby avoiding a worse fate?

As I pick up the dry gourd, I hear a faint rattle from trapped seeds, as though it is laughing with me at the memory of the fiasco Jonah made of what should have been a mission of love and good-will.

Arriving at Nineveh, a city so large that it took three days to travel on foot from one end to the other, and almost impregnable, surrounded as it was by walls a hundred feet high, Jonah lost no time in sounding his warning. When he was only one day's journey within the walls, he began preaching his message of doom to all who would listen: "Yet [only] forty days and Nineveh shall be overthrown!"

Over and over he declared the message so positively and perhaps eloquently, that he was accepted as a prophet from God and believed. The word spread quickly and panic gripped the whole city. Even the ruling powers took cognizance of the warning, an official decree being published ordering the city to go into mourning. Men and beasts were forbidden to take food for the forty-day period.

The heathen king evidenced a greater understanding of Jonah's God than did Jonah himself, for the decree also said, "Let man and beast be covered with sackcloth and cry mightily unto God; yea, let them turn every one from his evil way and from the violence that is in their hands. Who can tell if God will . . . turn away from his fierce anger, that we perish not?"

What more success could Jonah have asked than that an entire city fast and pray as a result of his warning? Yet he was far from happy about it. He seems to have been completely stunned when the forty-day period ended and nothing disastrous happened. The relieved people joyfully broke their long fast, laid aside their sackcloth (signs of mourning), and resumed normal activities, firmly convinced that God had spared them because of their repentance.

Jonah felt betrayed by God. He now feared he would either be scorned as a false prophet or scoffed at for having no true insight into God's plans, for he had not offered the people any hope. How could he, convinced as he was that the Jews alone were favored of God?

He saw the escape of the Ninevites as an act of divine mercy, and this only added to his misery. Reminding himself and God that he should have known God would repent and make a fool of him, he actually prayed to die, so deep was his humiliation. "Therefore now, O Lord, take, I beseech thee, my life from me, for it is better for me to die than to live."

God never answers such prayers, so nothing happened to Jonah. Then he began to be hopeful that the destruction he had predicted might yet happen. He decided to go outside the city walls to insure his own safety as well as to avoid the ridicule he feared. There he made himself a "booth," probably from dry boughs of trees, and sat in its meager shade to wait and "see what would become of the city."

But God's love went out to Jonah in his misery, and He caused the miraculous growth of a gourd vine. Overnight it grew so thick and long it provided a covering for Jonah's crude "booth," protecting him from the intense heat of the sun.

His shelter proved to be only temporary. A worm, also prepared by God, we are told, ate through the vine so that it died. Then again Jonah was defenseless against the heat, now intensified by a swelteringly hot wind, also prepared by God. When the sun rose high and beat upon Jonah's unprotected head, he fainted. Again he wished for death to end his misery.

Then God spoke to him, asking if he felt justified in being angry that the gourd vine was killed, and Jonah replied, doubtless vehemently, that he was.

To that the Lord replied, "Thou hast had pity on the gourd, for which thou hast not labored, neither madest it grow. . . . And should not I spare Nineveh, that great city wherein are more than sixscore thousand persons that cannot discern between their right hand and their left hand?"

Some historians say that Jonah is a fictional character, and that the short book bearing his name is an allegory written about 300 B.C. to protest Israel's stubborn refusal to believe God was interested in any but the Jewish nation. Other authorities dispute this conclusion. But whether real or imaginary, his story fictitious or true, seems unimportant. The lesson is real and dramatically presented.

In the shining surface of my inherited gourd, polished by time, I see mirrored countless faces from past ages. They are from every walk of life, all reflecting the joy and thanksgiving that Jonah must have seen in the faces of the Ninevites when they accepted as theirs the protective Power Jonah had considered exclusively his and his country's. Those faces seem to speak to me, challenging me with questions.

Am I willing to share my God's love with all men? Or do I exclude those who offend me, who do not measure up to my social or cultural standards? Do I really care what happens to others? Or am I smugly content in a booth of self-righteousness I have built for myself, waiting, like Jonah, to see what will become of the city?

Jonah's vine died, but my gourd must not. It symbolizes the inclusion of all men in the love that is in the Creator-God. He is a God with power to make a protective shelter from the elements and from the violence and injustice of men; with power to take away that shelter if spiritual maturity cannot be achieved with it.

Without the shelter of God's gourd, evidence of His tender care, we will all faint, as did Jonah. Without His guidance we are as infants, unable to discern between our right hand and our left hand.

So I would perpetuate the message of my inherited gourd, for in it lies the hope that all nations, like ancient Nineveh, become united and be "covered with sackcloth and cry mightily unto God; yea, let them turn every one . . . from the violence that is in their hands. Who can tell if [but what] God will . . . turn away from his fierce anger [his estrangement from man] that we perish not?"

A PACKAGE OF CRUMBS

Since today's housewife can buy crumbs in any grocery store, this seems a worthless gift to cherish. Just stale bread crumbs? That's right, except they are not stale, even though nearly two thousand years old. These crumbs are connected with an important incident of Jesus' ministry, and so they retain their freshness forever.

Although bearing no resemblance to each other, and separated in time by several centuries, this gift and Jonah's gourd are symbolic of the same truth—that God's love reaches out to all men alike. He looks at hearts only, not at outward appearances.

The Bible reminds us that prejudice toward other peoples began many centuries ago, and that it will continue until all human hearts are completely purified with divine love. At the time of the

Exodus, intolerance among the Israelites was a problem Moses had to cope with. Even though they were themselves being rescued from slavery arising from discrimination, the persecuted had become the persecutors. By the time of Jesus and long after the Resurrection, the problem continued.

Among the Jews of Palestine intolerance was especially strong toward Samaritans and Greeks. Doubtless the Romans were just as despised, but for political reasons the Jews were compelled to pretend a degree of tolerance for them as the rulers of Palestine. Even so, no self-respecting Jew socialized with Gentiles of any nationality.

Naturally the disciples were filled with this intolerance, and it was not until after the Crucifixion and Pentecost that they began to accept the universality of God. Then Peter and Paul met great resistance among followers of the New Way when they pioneered in taking the Gospel to Gentiles.

Jesus, who was completely free of prejudice, met this problem as he did all those arising from the weakness of men: with love and tolerance and patience. This was evidenced at the time a woman spoke to him about the crumbs that became a part of our Biblical inheritance.

Because he went wherever he was received, and his disciples went wherever he did, this incident happened in Syria, near the coastal towns of Tyre and Sidon. Jesus needed rest from the crowds that followed him wherever he went, and sought seclusion to find it. Mark 7 tells us he "entered into an house and would have no man know it; but he could not be hid."

No doubt the devoted disciples stood guard at the door of the house while Jesus rested, and it is here that the story of my crumbs begins. A Syrophoenician mother came that day to ask for healing of her daughter who she said was possessed with devils.

As we have seen, any nervous or mental disorder at the time was believed to be an indication the victim was under the power of Satanic forces, so we do not know the nature of the daughter's illness. It must have been very serious to drive the mother to the point where she would ask help of a Jew such as Jesus was known to be, and to get past the watchful disciples. This she did, for she "came and fell at his feet . . . and she besought him that he would cast forth the devil out of her daughter."

How desperate she must have been to dare hope a Jewish Healer would care about the afflicted daughter of a despised Greek, whose people were commonly referred to by Jews as "dogs"! What faith, to believe he could exercise his power without even seeing the child! Jesus must surely have been touched by faith like that, yet he met her first pleas with stony silence.

We can be sure, however, that he had a purpose in appearing indifferent. Perhaps it was to test the mother's faith, or to teach the disciples a lesson, or both. Knowing hearts as he did, he must have been aware that the mother would not be easily rebuffed, that she would suffer any humiliation on the chance that her beloved child might be helped.

Jesus knew—but his disciples did not. They only knew that this Gentile woman was brash, unforgivably bold, in forcing herself upon a Jew of Jesus' importance, and they must have all but barred her way to Jesus. That did not settle anything, for she refused to go away. Despairing of her, they enlisted the help of Jesus in getting rid of her.

"Send her away," they implored him, "for she crieth after us."

We would expect Jesus to reprove those impatient disciples, all of whom had dedicated their lives to the advancement of God's Kingdom. Yet he did not. Why? The question is often asked.

It may have been because he preferred to make his reproof that of precedent instead of words, as is generally assumed. Or could it not be that he felt no reproof in his heart? He knew full well what deep roots such prejudice had, centuries and centuries deep. He loved all men, but he did not measure his love by their virtues, nor did he love his disciples less that they adhered to the teachings in which they had been reared.

He probably told them to bring the woman back to him, knowing as he must have that they confidently expected to see her ordered to leave and not trouble them further. Earlier they had been pleased to hear him say to her, "I am not sent but unto the lost sheep of the house of Israel."

Jesus' next words to her were a reminder of the low regard in which Jews held her people. Or was not the reminder for the disciples, making them aware that he knew the thoughts of their hearts? When she knelt before him and again prayed, "Lord [sir] help me," we are told he answered, speaking directly to her this time, "It is not meet [right] to take the children's bread and cast it to the dogs."

Few of her people would have heard this hated expression without feeling and showing resentment. The Greeks were as proud as the Jews, and this mother had already been subjected to great humiliation that day. Yet her reply to this seeming insult came quickly and humbly, even humorously, indicating there was no malice in her heart: "Truth, Lord; yet the dogs eat of the crumbs which fall from their masters' table."

Was she merely being politic, saying what she thought would please Jesus, a Jew? Perhaps the disciples thought so, but apparently Jesus did not. "He said unto her, O woman, great is thy faith, be it unto thee even as thou wilt."

Then, we may be sure, the disciples did not need to urge her to leave. Mark writes that Jesus told her, "For this saying, go thy way; the devil is gone out of thy daughter." Words like that must certainly have sent a weary and despairing mother hurrying home to her daughter, a song of joy and thanksgiving in her heart. Did it matter at all that her daughter's healing had come about through One of a despised people? Only the healing was important, and plainly she accepted that as already accomplished or she would not have left.

Would she not have been humanly justified to go in doubt and misgiving, not sure how much she could trust the word of a Jew? Because she was free of such doubts and had a purified heart, she found, upon arriving at her home, her daughter lying quietly on the bed, no longer tormented by the "demons."

Opening my package in retrospect, I let the crumbs fall through my fingers, each scrap a reminder of such tragedies as inbred hatreds and resentments, bitterness and distrust and warped lives. The crumbs also remind me that the power of love can liberate minds and inspire a trust that is mutual and therefore operative.

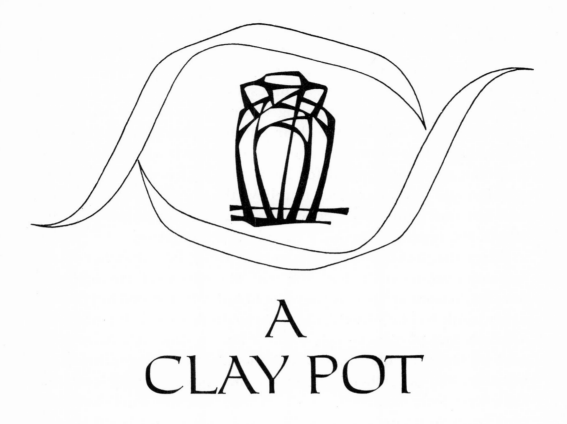

A
CLAY POT

Recently a museum of anthropology in my state of Arizona displayed some early Indian artifacts among which was a beautifully preserved clay vessel that paleontologists estimate was made centuries before the time of Christ.

In my prized collection of inherited Bible objects is such a clay vessel, dating back to the time of Elisha, the beloved baldheaded prophet who succeeded the great Elijah. This clay pot once held the precious olive oil that provided both fuel and food for the people of that day.

Poverty has been a social evil as far back as history records. The woman who used my oil container was the poorest of the poor, economically speaking. She was a widow with two young sons and no means of support. Even worse, she faced the imminent possibility of seeing her boys taken as slaves to pay her deceased husband's debts. That was trouble indeed!

Although her story (2 Kings 4) is extraordinary, it illustrates truth so graphically that she assumes a very real identity for many people today who are struggling to break the chains of poverty that they fear will enslave their children. During her time the widow had no government agencies or benevolent organizations to which she could appeal for help, no banks or loan companies which might advance money to relieve the pressures of debts. She had but one glimmer of hope. She went to the prophet Elisha, whom she regarded as God's earthly representative.

When the prophet heard her pitiful story, he asked her if she had any resources. She had, she said, one pot of oil. He then gave her instructions so strange they would today be ignored or rejected as an insult to one's intelligence. He told her to go out among the villagers and borrow vessels ("not a few"), which she was to fill with oil from her one small pot. Although this seemed utterly impossible, she nevertheless accepted the challenge with childlike faith that brought about a miracle. She and her sons borrowed pots from all their neighbors. Then the widow shut her door and poured oil from her one pot into the many empty containers, for the oil continued to flow from her own small pot as long as her two sons brought her empty vessels to receive it. When she told Elisha what had happened, he said, "Go, sell the oil and pay thy debt, and live thou and thy children of the rest."

Thus my hereditary clay pot symbolizes the inexhaustible flow of God's love where there is faith in hearts to receive it. Those hearts must be empty of everything but love and faith.

My little pot is a reminder that God cannot solve economic problems without cooperation on our part. The widow was not told by Elisha to go home and wait for help to be sent her. She was told to do something to relieve her situation. More than that, she was told to put her sons to work, to expect them to share in her responsibilities and in her faith. There were no corroding fears, no crippling despondency or self-pity, no fixed ideas of how God's help must come or how it cannot come.

The task she assigned the boys was not an easy one. By going abroad boldly they risked being seized for debt by their creditor who was probably just waiting to catch them alone and defenseless. They invited ridicule and humiliation in asking to borrow vessels to receive oil they did not have. Their confidence, however, must have been enough to impress their friends and neighbors, for their mission was accomplished. They went in faith instead of in fear.

This crude clay pot, the product of what is thought of as a primitive culture, I lovingly bequeath to all troubled and burdened mothers. It may help them realize that children are not kept free through overprotectiveness or indulgence; that there can be no free bodies except where there are free spirits.

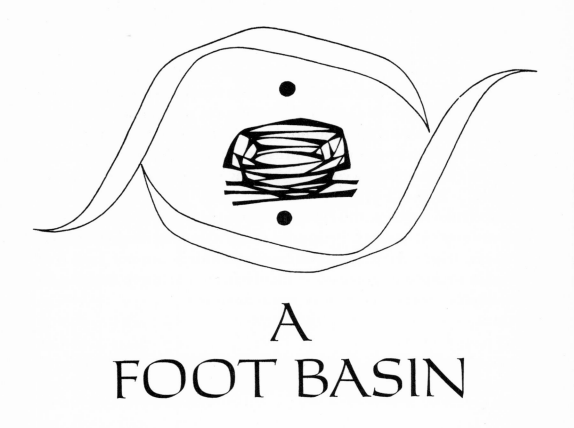

A
FOOT BASIN

One of the recollections of childhood is of the gaily flowered china washbowl and pitcher that preceded modern bathrooms. Such sets are prized as antiques today, and it is with great pride that I display a far older wash basin in my Biblical collection.

It is not of china, nor does it have any decorative touches. Yet it is more beautiful than any to be found in antique shops, for it was once used by our Lord to wash the feet of his disciples. That makes it sacred and worthy of a place of honor in my exhibit.

Washing the feet of guests was a social custom at the time of Jesus, the implication being that the host considered himself inferior to his guests and thus honored them through such service. Sometimes servants performed the actual rites, but special guests received the host's personal attention to express his high esteem.

According to the account in John's Gospel, Jesus used my basin to honor his disciples at the famous Last Supper. At this meal in an upper room of the home which was possibly that of young Mark and his widowed mother, Jesus surprised his disciples by laying aside his outer clothing, girding his waist with a towel, pouring water into a basin, and then proceeding to wash their feet in turn. No doubt the first ones were too surprised to protest, but when he came to Simon Peter, he met with firm resistance.

"Lord," Peter said, "dost thou wash my feet?" (Perhaps he added, "It is more fitting that I should wash yours.")

Jesus replied, "What I do thou knowest [understandeth] not now; but thou shalt know hereafter."

Probably feeling that Jesus was demeaning himself, Peter said vehemently, "Thou shalt never wash my feet."

Impetuous, lovable Peter, too worshipful of his Leader to accept such menial service from him! In his love he doubtless wanted to be the one to serve. Is this not always true? Is not love like that?

As I continue to look at my wash basin, generally conceded to be an emblem of true humility as demonstrated by our Savior, I am struck by another thought. Jesus' act was inspired not by humility, but by love, love longing to give, to serve, to express itself in deeds as well as in words. The disciples seemed obtusely unaware of his yearning love on the eve of his betrayal and crucifixion.

Understanding came to Peter when he heard Jesus' reply: "If I wash thee not, thou hast no part with me."

If I wash thee not. If I am not allowed to serve you, he was saying, you are rejecting my love. I must give in order to fulfill the law of love. Even though he knew that within a matter of hours he would give his life for the world, he wanted this opportunity to demonstrate that his gift was personal, to show that his was more than a general love for all mankind.

A verse of Scripture comes to mind. It is found in Isaiah 43:1: "I [the Lord God] have called thee by thy name; thou art mine."

Then, feeling as though divine hands touched my own feet lovingly, I bow my head and whisper Peter's reply to Jesus' conditions: "Lord, [wash] not my feet only, but also my hands and my head."

So much is said about the service we owe God, the service He rightfully expects of those who call themselves Christian. So little is said about the service God longs to show us. He is love, we say. But do we forget that love asks to give, not to receive? To serve, not to be served? Do we not reject divine love when we accept limitations in our lives? Do we not also reject it when we practice a false humility by giving and doing so much for others in His name, while protesting over receiving anything for ourselves?

It is neither true unselfishness nor true humility to find pleasure in giving and yet deny that same pleasure to either God or man.

That night long ago, when my Savior washed the feet of the Twelve in an upper room in Jerusalem, he also washed mine. He took the role of servant that men might see the true nature of love. His heart was overflowing with it that night, and saddened because his love was being rejected. In the previous months many people had followed him for "the loaves and fishes," hoping for selfish gain; many had accepted his healing, seeing in it a miraculous expression of power. But, looking at my ancient vessel, I wonder how many recognized love in his miracles. How many really felt close to the Man himself? How many today feel that personal bond between themselves and the Son of God?

My foot basin also reminds me that the supper in the upper room, the ceremony of washing, and the words of Jesus (inscribed on John's heart as if by fire) did not climax that memorable night. It was climaxed in Gethsemane, a garden on the Mount of Olives, which was a retreat for those desiring solitude for meditation and prayer. To this garden Jesus and the disciples, with the exception of Judas, retired at the close of the supper hour.

It was climaxed by desertion of all the disciples. Although they had listened to words from his lips, the words were still too deep for their understanding. Too deep, because at that point they did not understand love with all its attributes; did not yet know the greatness and the fullness of God's love for men.

If they had, could they have slept while he suffered? Could they have run at sight of the soldiers, led by temple guards? Could Peter, who only a short time before was volubly protesting his love and loyalty and declaring vehemently, "Lord, I will lay down my life for thy sake!" have "followed afar off," and even later deny knowing his Master? The time came when Peter did understand and did lay down his life for Christ, but that night, although he did not betray his Master to the authorities, as did Judas, he failed Jesus completely.

Judas sold his Master for money, but all the disciples failed him, all deserted him, through fear for themselves.

Is Gethsemane ended? This is a question my wash basin seems to ask. Do not those who call themselves his disciples still fail Jesus? Many of us "betray" him daily for money—not just by withholding gifts, nor by our desire to make money, but by giving it all-importance when we do not have it. Worrying over lack of money is a denial of his protective love.

All of us prove faithless to him daily through fear. The disciples cannot be censured by us, for they thought they had good reason to run for their lives that night. Temporarily they forgot the power they had seen demonstrated by their Leader, forgot he had fed an army of people with only two fishes and a few loaves of bread, had healed incurable diseases and even raised the dead. They deserted through panic, betrayed into forgetfulness through fear.

How different are we? Are not some of us chronic worriers? Do we not panic when serious illness or trouble threatens our loved ones or ourselves? If we fail to meet our troubles with courage or if there is daily less than joy in our hearts, we are following our Master afar off as did Peter that eventful night. We are, in effect, denying to the world that we even know him. Either that, or our faithless actions proclaim that God is powerless or even dead, as some claim.

While men question the reality of God, are not most of us sleeping? Are we even aware that Christ sweats drops of blood in his agony over man's inhumanity to man?

Because I, too, have so often followed Christ afar off, I would bequeath my foot basin to the fearful Christian, whatever the reasons for the fears that keep him from realizing the glorious freedom that is the heritage of our faith.

Let my basin remind you of words Jesus spoke in his great Sermon on the Mount: "What man is there of you, whom if his son ask bread, will he give him a stone? Or if he ask a fish, will he give him a serpent? If ye then, being evil [weak humans] know how to give good gifts unto your children, how much more shall your Father which is in heaven give good things to them that ask him?"

God is love and love longs to give. The one gift He asks from us is trust in that love and in His power. Any other service we render Him is giving to ourselves, to our spiritual development and the betterment of the world in which we live.

So, together with this gift symbolizing divine love, I would add six words Jesus spoke that night at the Last Supper. The words should be potent for Christians living in these troubled times, as they have proved to be highly effective for believers in countless other troubled eras. They are, "Let not your hearts be troubled."

A
SILVER CUP

Almost all who recall preplastic days remember the small silver mugs from which children used to drink their milk. Such a mug today is often cherished as a potential family heirloom.

In my Biblical collection there is a silver cup that once belonged to a young Hebrew named Joseph, living several generations before Moses. It has a special significance for it stands for the spirit of forgiveness—the outstanding characteristic of its original owner. In bequeathing his cup to posterity he also passed along the obligation to forgive those who bring hurt or wrong.

Obligation is perhaps not the right word. Privilege is more apropos, for the one who forgives is the one who is rewarded. The heart that harbors unforgiveness closes the door against God, who makes Himself known through love. Since love and resentment are directly opposed to each other, there can be no harmony where both exist.

Psychiatrists and psychologists today see deep-rooted resentments and guilt (unforgiveness of self) as the cause of many mental and bodily ills. Forgiveness may often have been ostensibly given, yet the memory retained the hurt. Like a deeply buried root, it held life enough to continue to spread the poison of malice and hate.

All over the world in every language prayers for peace continue to be said. Philosophers for centuries have been reminding us that peace must begin with the individual. The early prophet Isaiah wrote (26:3): "Thou wilt keep him in perfect peace, whose mind is stayed on thee."

Judging by the social unrest, the crime rate increase, and the spirit of violence abroad in many lands, this individual peace seems far from being achieved. Since every attitude, even one's inmost thoughts, contributes to the spirit of the times, each individual bears a unique responsibility. Each of us might well look within to measure the peace in his own heart.

How can this personal peace be achieved under present-day conditions? The young Hebrew slave who once owned my cup answered the question thousands of years ago, not in words, but in his fascinating life story as recorded in Genesis, chapters 37 through 50.

Joseph, eldest of two sons of Jacob by his beloved wife, Rachel, incurred the bitter resentment of his ten half-brothers because of Jacob's open display of favoritism to him. When their father sent the youth to join his older brothers as they guarded the family's flocks in the hills, they became enraged to see him wearing a colorful new coat given him by his father. They seized Joseph and threw him into a deep pit. He was rescued by some Midianites, who in turn sold him to a nomadic tribe. Eventually he was taken into Egypt and sold as a slave to a captain in the army of Pharoah.

Potiphar, Joseph's new master, quickly became so attached to the alert, handsome youth that he made him overseer of his household, trusting him so completely that Potiphar "knew not aught he had save the bread which he did eat."

Trouble developed because the captain was not the only one attracted to the young Hebrew slave. Potiphar's determined and scheming wife began to make bold advances, finally forcing Joseph to repulse her rather than betray his master's trust. Humiliated and furious over her rejection, the woman took revenge upon Joseph by staging a scene calculated to be witnessed by the other servants, and declaring that Joseph had tried to force his attentions upon her.

Because Potiphar believed his wife's accusation to be true, Joseph could not defend himself. Thrown into prison by his outraged owner, he spent two years in a dark dungeon. This is the background of a story too long to detail. The part that interests us now is Joseph's attitude of forgiveness and his rewards for such an attitude.

Through his powers of divination and gift for interpreting dreams, Joseph eventually came to the attention of Pharaoh. The latter, impressed with his business acumen, gave him his freedom and the position of governor of Egypt, second in authority only to the king himself.

Through this series of circumstances the treacherous brothers of Joseph eventually came under his power. There was a drought and subsequent famine in both Egypt and Israel, but Joseph's wise conservation program as governor had kept plenty of grain in Egypt's storehouses. Hearing of this supply of food, Jacob sent his sons to bargain for some.

Joseph now was in a position to seek revenge. But he held no ill will against his brothers. He did, however, hesitate to rely on the integrity of men who had once betrayed their father's trust, making him believe that wild animals had killed his favorite son. Joseph therefore tested them (of course they had failed to recognize their brother in this high official) by having his servant hide a silver cup in the grain sack of Benjamin, his own full-blood brother and the youngest and most favored son of Jacob at that time.

As soon as the brothers started back to Israel with their purchase of grain, messengers were sent to overtake them. After searching their sacks and finding the cup, they charged Benjamin with theft and demanded that he return with them to pay for his crime by becoming the servant of Joseph, the governor.

With the evidence against him, none of the brothers could have doubted Benjamin's guilt. Nor could they have doubted the gravity of his offense, for not only was the cup valuable for its precious metal, but also because it was used by Joseph in practicing the ancient art of hydromancy, or divination. Yet as one man they insisted upon returning with the messengers to plead Benjamin's cause.

When the eleven men were brought before Joseph, Judah, the oldest and the one responsible for Joseph's betrayal, pleaded to take Benjamin's place. The loss of his beloved youngest son, he declared, might hasten the death of their aged father. Joseph's scheme had the desired result. Upon seeing the sign of repentance in Judah, and proof of his love for their father, Joseph joyfully made himself known to them. In offering his brothers forgiveness he also exonerated them of the sin that must have lain heavily on the conscience of each.

"Be not grieved, nor angry with yourselves," he told them, adding that they had actually been instruments of God in working out their own destiny. "God sent me before you to preserve you . . . and to save your lives by a great deliverance. So now it was not you that sent me hither, but God."

Joseph's remark expressed true forgiveness. It came from the heart willingly, joyfully, and so completely that no seeds of resentment could possibly have remained. The cleansing process was simple and yet entirely effective: he stopped looking back at evil and saw good.

The story also illustrates that the mind does not have to forget wrongs, but merely to remember them without emotion, without adverse judgment. Even though Joseph had forgiven his brothers, he did not forget that they had shown themselves unworthy of trust. By releasing them to God, he could look at their human errors with detachment. Then forgiveness was complete.

In bequeathing this lovely silver cup to others, therefore, I add the hope that it may awaken the need for the individual peace that comes with forgiveness, the inner peace so essential for constructive living.

A
SPONGE

Along with my silver cup, this sponge found in the New Testament also suggests forgiveness and is, beyond doubt, the most precious of all the gifts I have placed on display.

Can an ordinary sponge measure up to this claim? This one can, for it once ministered to my crucified Savior. Paradoxically, it did not give him comfort or help. Rather, it added to his suffering. It is precious not because of the acrid vinegar it once conveyed to his bleeding lips, but because of the spirit in which he received that final cruelty.

Jesus already had suffered so many cruelties! He had been beaten until his body was striped with great broken welts; a crown of sharp thorns had been pressed down on his head and brow until blood streaked his face; he had been driven like a dumb animal through the streets of Jerusalem, bowed under the weight of the cross to which he would be nailed.

He had been cursed and spat upon, mocked and jeered and laughed at. He had had his arms stretched across the crossbars and nails driven through his palms and feet. The great cross was then lifted up until finally he hung there on the hill, his head and naked body exposed to the blistering heat of the sun.

Yet, through all the tortures Jesus showed only forgiveness for his persecutors. "Father, forgive them, for they know not what they do," he prayed in his anguish. A heart of love such as his could hold no thoughts of resentment, of retribution, or even of self-pity. His pity was for his enemies, because they had no love, no mercy, no God in their hearts.

When, near the end of his suffering, his feverish thirst became unendurable and he asked for a drink, my sponge, soaked in vinegar, was tied to the end of a reed and lifted to his parched lips. The four Gospel writers mention the sponge. For me it seems symbolic of the love and forgiveness of Jesus' life and death.

Some historians believe that the vinegar offered Jesus (generally agreed to be a sour wine) contained a merciful opiate to relieve his intense pain. Yet there was no mercy in the crowd that watched my Lord die. With the exception of several women who loved him, and at least one disciple, all of whom were helpless to do anything for him, the crowd had come to watch a man suffer the most cruel death human brutishness could inflict.

Scenes of the crucifixion flash before my eyes as I go back through time to stand, horror-stricken, on a barren, rocky hillside. A mother sobs beside me—and I can find no words with which to comfort her. I look into a disciple's dazed eyes—and can feel his bewildered agony. I share the grief and desolation of a friend called Mary Magdalene—whose whole life was transformed by having known the Man now dying before her.

Then I notice two men who are not a part of the crowd. They hang on crosses on either side of Jesus, common thieves paying the penalty decreed such lawbreakers by the Roman government. It was the same punishment meted out to Jesus.

Something more than curiosity moves me to watch three men instead of one. I find myself becoming intensely interested in how a thief faces death. Or is it myself I am watching? Am I not a thief also? Have I not stolen time that belongs to God? Robbed Him of honor by an unproductive life? Cheated Him of praise He should have had?

It suddenly seems easier to identify with thieves than with the weeping women. In retrospect I am part of the drama of Calvary, a drama that happened over nineteen hundred years ago, and I have a leading role. Am I not all men?

I notice that one of the dying thieves is looking at Jesus on the center cross. He appears to be only a little older than Jesus' thirty-three years, but a wasted life has left its mark upon his gaunt body and dissipated face. In the pain-wrenched eyes I seem to see wonder that the Nazarene can endure the same suffering so quietly.

From the ground comes raucous laughter and jeering cries. "He saved others; let him save himself, if he be Christ."

The lips of the dying Jesus move, and I feel that one of the thieves hears his whispered prayer for his tormentors. Does the thief also see the holy light that I perceive upon the face of my Lord? I wonder, and a moment later have my answer. It comes when the other thief, hardly more than a youth but with a hard, arrogant face, starts to berate Jesus, as though to find release for the explosions of pain in his own body.

"If thou be Christ, save thyself and us," he taunts, taking up the jeers of the crowd. It is then that the first thief replies to my unspoken question by answering the mocking thief, "Dost not thou fear God, seeing thou art in the same condemnation? And we indeed justly, for we receive the due reward of our deeds; but this man hath done nothing amiss."

Then, I am thrilled to see the thief who defended Jesus turn his head toward him and say, "Lord, remember me when thou comest into thy kingdom."

It is at once a confession of faith and a prayer for forgiveness. True, it is what might be termed a deathbed repentance, but it is not rejected by Jesus. When did God ever reject one who turns to Him?

With a vibrant note of love in his voice, Jesus answers the repentant thief: "Verily I say unto thee, Today shalt thou be with me in paradise." At this instant the thief discerns the flash of a radiant smile, as bright as the sun, upon the face of Jesus.

Before long the vinegar-soaked sponge is put on a reed and given to Jesus to drink, and a voice challenges, "Let us see whether Elias will come to take him down."

After Jesus receives the vinegar, he says, "It is finished." His head bows and he dies.

The thieves are dying more slowly. Sundown approaches and with it the beginning of the Sabbath when bodies must not remain upon the cross, so the soldiers break the limbs of the thieves in order to hasten their death.

Jesus' limbs they do not break, they only pierce his side, because his sagging head and body indicate that he is already dead. The repentant thief and I know they are wrong, for a radiance streams from the center cross. And out of that glory I seem to see an extended hand, reaching, reaching, toward a thief—toward someone like myself.

Still watching the thief to whom Jesus gave the promise of redemption, I note that the lines of pain in his face are suddenly smoothed, as though touched by angelic hands. A great exultation rises in me, for I know that I am witnessing victory—victory over death.

As though they, too, had caught a glimpse of the glory upon the hill of Calvary, the crowd moves away silently. For some the fun is over. For others a dream is dead. A centurion, captain of the Roman soldiers detailed to carry out the execution, lingers a moment, staring at the figure on the center cross and murmuring, "Truly this man was the Son of God."

A man called Joseph of Arimathaea, who had secretly believed in

Jesus but lacked the moral courage to say so publicly, has come to claim the body of Jesus, having asked permission of Pilate to place it in his own tomb. As I turn away from the scene, I see a reed lying on the ground where it has been cast aside by the soldiers. On the end is attached a sponge soaked in vinegar.

Or is it vinegar? The dying light turns the sponge red, as though soaked in blood, and makes it beautiful. Beautiful because it represents not man's crime in crucifying his Lord, but his great heart of love that could so readily forgive.

A precious gift like this must be carefully preserved if the world is ever to know peace. Although I would like to bequeath my sponge to hearts ready to receive it and value it, I know that that is not what Christ Jesus would have me do.

He would ask me to leave it to those who have wasted their lives as had the two who died with him—lives that belong to him; to those who can watch indifferently, or jeer, while others die to make a better world; to those who, like Pilate, wash their hands of responsibility and let Christianity be crucified; to those who, like Joseph of Arimathaea, secretly believe but consider it poor policy to say so; and to those whose hearts are too hardened to believe.

Above all, I think, he would have the sponge which symbolizes his love given to those who carry his banner, but deny him power; who praise his Name but live as though he had never been born.

Jesus would not, however, want the sponge soaked in acrid wine or vinegar to be given even to his enemies. He would ask that it be fresh, cool water to quench their thirst.

He is like that.